STUDY GUIDE

Gwendolyn M. Parsons

Abnormal Psychology in a Changing World

FIFTH EDITION

Jeffrey S. Nevid, Ph.D.

St. John's University

Spencer A. Rathus, Ph.D.

New York University

Beverly Greene, Ph.D.

St. John's University

Prentice Hall, Upper Saddle River, New Jersey 07458

© 2003 by PEARSON EDUCATION, INC.
Upper Saddle River, New Jersey 07458

ISBN 0-13-049508-5

Printed in the United States of America

TABLE OF CONTENTS

Chapter One

Introduction and Methods of Research

OBJECTIVES

1. Discuss six criteria that are used to define abnormal behavior.
2. Discuss the relationship between cultural beliefs and norms and the labeling of behavior as normal or abnormal.
3. Recount the history of beliefs about disturbed behavior and treatment of people deemed "mad" or mentally ill.
4. Discuss the following contemporary perspectives on abnormal behavior: biological, psychodynamic, learning based, humanistic, cognitive, and sociocultural.
5. Discuss the steps involved in the scientific method.
6. Explain how experimenters control for subjects' and researchers' expectations and the differences between three types of experimental validity.
7. Discuss the various methods used to study abnormal behavior, including the naturalistic observation method, the correlational method, the experimental method, kinship studies, the epidemiological method, and the case study method.

CHAPTER OUTLINE

How Do We Define Abnormal Behavior?
    Criteria for Determining Abnormality
    Cultural Bases of Abnormal Behavior
Historical Perspectives on Abnormal Behavior
    The Demonological Model
    Origins of the Medical Model: In "Ill Humor"
    Medieval Times
    Witchcraft
    Asylums
    The Reform Movement and Moral Therapy
    A Step Backward
    The Community Mental Health Movement: The Exodus from State Hospitals
    Contemporary Perspectives on Abnormal Behavior: From Demonology to Science
Research Methods in Abnormal Psychology
    Description, Explanation, Prediction, and Control: The Objectives of Science
    The Scientific Method
    Ethics in Research
    The Naturalistic-Observation Method
    Correlation
    The Experimental Method
    Experimental Validity
    Epidemiological Method
    Kinship Studies
    The Case-Study Method
Summing Up

MATCHING

Answers are found at the end of this chapter. Match these terms and concepts with the definitions that follow:

abnormal psychology
psychologist
medical model
monozygotic twins
case study
correlation
internal validity
construct validity
informed consent
prevalence
blind
unobtrusive
independent variable
dependent variable
scientific method
phenothiazines
deinstitutionalization
worldview
delusion
placebo

psychological disorders
experimental subjects
critical thinking
dizygotic twins
sample
causal
external validity
longitudinal study
theory
incidence
experimental method
positive correlation
negative correlation
moral therapy
catharsis
trephening
hypnosis
description
psychodynamic model
significant

1. _____ the 19th century treatment approach that emphasized treating hospitalized patients with care and understanding

2. _____ a person with advanced graduate training in psychology

3. _____ part of a population

4. _____ purgation of feelings

5. _____ cause and effect

6. _____ a relationship between variables

7. _____ a magnitude of difference that indicates meaningful differences between groups

8. _____ the number of new cases of a disorder that occurs within a specific period of time

9. _____ subjects who are given the experimental treatment in an experiment

10. _____ an objective of science, it is based upon careful observation of behavior

11. _____ a state of being unaware of whether one has received the experimental treatment

12. _____ a model; indicates laws and principles underlying behaviors

13. _____ a statistical relationship between two variables such that increases in one are associated with increases in the other

14. _____ a type of correlational study whereby subjects are followed over time

15. _____ the overall number of cases of a disorder in a population within a specific period of time

16. _____ variable that is measured in an experiment

17. _____ the degree to which treatments effects can be accounted for by the theoretical constructs represented in the independent variables

18. _____ not interfering

19. _____ the theoretical model of Freud and his followers, in which abnormal behavior is viewed as the product of clashing forces within the personality

20. _____ a series of steps used to answer questions based on empirical evidence

21. _____ the practice of discharging psychiatric patients from hospitals into the community

22. _____ a perspective in which abnormal behavior is viewed as symptomatic of underlying illnesses or disorders

23. _____ abnormal behavior patterns that involve a disturbance of psychological functioning or behavior

24. _____ a prehistoric practice of cutting a hole in a person's skull

25. _____ the branch of psychology that deals with the description, causes, and treatment of abnormal behavior patterns

26. _____ a questioning attitude about information you hear or read

27. _____ twins that develop from the same fertilized egg

28. _____ a carefully drawn biography based on clinical interviews, observations, and psychological tests

29. _____ twins that develop from separate fertilized eggs

30. _____ the principle that subjects should receive enough information about an experiment beforehand to decide freely whether or not to participate

31. _____ the degree to which experimental results can be generalized to other settings and conditions

32. _____ an inert medication or bogus treatment that is intended to control for expectancy effects

33. _____ a statistical relationship between two variables such that increases in one are associated with decreases in the other

34. _____ a firmly held but unfounded belief or idea that persists despite evidence that it has no basis in reality

35. _____ a prevailing view of the times

36. _____ a scientific method that aims to discover causal relationships

37. _____ the variable that is manipulated in an experiment

38. _____ a group of antipsychotic drugs used to treat schizophrenia

39. _____ a state induced by suggestion; Charcot used this for the treatment of hysteria

40. _____ the degree to which manipulation of the independent variables can be causally related to changes in the dependent variables

CROSSWORD

Answers are found at the end of this chapter. Complete the following crossword puzzle to reinforce your understanding of this chapter's key terms and concepts:

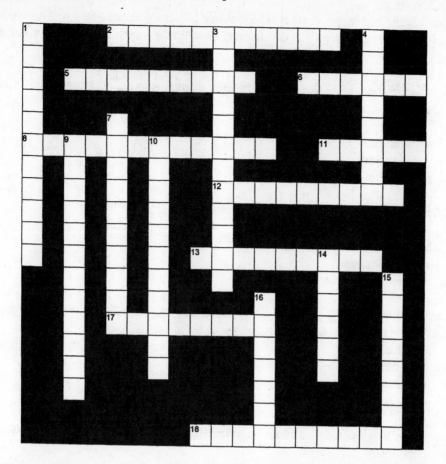

ACROSS	
2.	relationship between variables
5.	variable that is measured in an experiment
6.	cause and effect
8.	method that aims to discover causal relationships
11.	state of being unaware of whether one has received the experimental treatment
12.	to be fully informed about an experiment after it has taken place
13.	purgation of feelings
17.	type of validity/degree to which experimental results can be generalized to other settings
18.	an assumption that is tested through experimentation

DOWN	
1.	variable that is manipulated in an experiment
3.	type of correlational study
4.	type of correlation whereby increases in one variable are associated with increases in another
7.	overall number of cases of a disorder
9.	person with advanced graduate traing in psychology
10.	twins that develop from the same fertilized egg
14.	part of a population
15.	science of heredity
16.	an inert medication that is intended to control for expectancy effects

MULTIPLE CHOICE

Answers are found at the end of this chapter. The multiple choice questions listed will test your understanding of the material presented in the chapter. Read through each question and circle the letter representing the best answer.

1. The objective of the _____ research method is to uncover cause-and–effect relationships between variables.
   a. case study
   b. experimental
   c. correlational
   d. naturalistic-observational

2. Which is not required by multiple baseline designs?
   a. a reversal phase
   b. a treatment phase
   c. a baseline phase
   d. an intervention phase

3. Correlations allow for _____, but do not provide information regarding causal relationships between variables.
   a. informed studies
   b. prediction
   c. explanation
   d. causation

4. It is necessary that a research sample be representative of the _____ of interest.
   a. experiment
   b. population
   c. subject
   d. behavior

5. An experiment is designed to assess the effects of modeling on public speaking performance. In this design,
   a. modeling is the dependent variable and the independent variable.
   b. public speaking performance is the dependent variable and modeling is the independent variable.
   c. public speaking performance is the independent variable and modeling is the dependent variable.
   d. none of the above.

6. The extent to which experimental results may be generalized to other settings and conditions is referred to as
   a. internal validity.
   b. external validity.
   c. generalization.
   d. significant.

7. In a correlational study, Dr. Sanford discovered that as test scores increased for students the time spent watching television decreased. This would indicate a _____ correlation between the two variables.
    a. positive
    b. significant
    c. negative
    d. nonsignificant

8. Explanation of abnormal behavior in terms of supernatural forces is characteristic of the _____ model.
    a. psychodynamic
    b. demonological
    c. correlational
    d. moral treatment

9. Which of the following is not an objective of the scientific approach to abnormal psychology?
    a. description
    b. statistical analysis
    c. explanation
    d. control

10. A single subject research method in the form of an A-B-A-B design is called
    a. a longitudinal study.
    b. a case study.
    c. a multiple baseline design.
    d. a reversal design.

11. Which of the following is true of naturalistic observation?
    a. it provides considerable information about behavior but cannot specify why a behavior occurs.
    b. it is conducted through quasiexperiments.
    c. it frequently employs surveys.
    d. it is of little value for studying abnormal behavior.

12. In the early sixties, community mental health centers were given the responsibility of providing continuing support and care to former hospitalized patients under a policy of _____.
    a. moral therapy
    b. deinstitutionalization
    c. research
    d. drug treatment

13. A group of antipsychotic drugs, _____ permitted many patients with schizrenia to be discharged to less restrictive living arrangements and reduced the most flagrant behavior patterns associated with this disorder.
    a. phenothiazines
    b. humors
    c. serothiazines
    d. fluozines

14. The _____ model provided the first psychological perspective on abnormal behavior.
    a. biopsychsocial
    b. psychodynamic
    c. medical
    d. psychosomatic

15. The _____ involves systematic attempts to test our assumptions and theories about the world through gathering objective evidence.
    a. experimental model
    b. scientific method
    c. longitudinal method
    d. psychological model

16. Research subjects must be given enough information in advance about a study's purposes, methods, risks, and benefits to allow them to make a decision regarding their participation. This illustrates the principle of _____.
    a. sampling
    b. informed consent
    c. bias
    d. ethical treatment

17. The _____ allows scientists to demonstrate a causal relationship between variables.
    a. scientific method
    b. experimental method
    c. correlational method
    d. biopsychological method

18. In an experiment, _____ are not given the experimental treatment.
    a. baseline subjects
    b. independent variables
    c. dependent variables
    d. control subjects
    e. none of the above

19. In a _____ , neither the researcher nor the subject is told whether an active drug or placebo is being administered.
    a. single-subject research design
    b. double-blind placebo design
    c. single-blind placebo-control study
    d. reversal deign

20. If observed changes in the dependent variable can be causally related to the independent variable, an experiment is said to have _____.
    a. reliability
    b. internal validity
    c. external validity
    d. construct validity

21. Rates of occurrence of abnormal behavior in various settings or population groups are studied by use of the _____ method.
    a. scientific
    b. epidemiological
    c. correlational
    d. naturalistic-observational

22. Sam and Sue are identical twins. They are also known as _____.
    a. dizygotic
    b. correlated
    c. concordant
    d. monozygotic

23. Freud's in depth study of Leonardo da Vinci illustrates the use of the _____.
    a. experimental process
    b. case study method
    c. longitudinal method
    d. observational design

24. In an A-B-A-B design , the experimenter can be confident the treatment had the intended effect if
    a. the behavior improves whenever treatment is introduced, but returns to baseline levels during the reversal phase.
    b. the behavior improves during the reversal phase, but returns during treatment conditions.
    c. the behavior improves across experimental and control conditions.
    d. none of the above.

25. While reading about a psychological disorder on the internet, Sally began to question the accuracy and credibility of the information presented. This illustrates her use of _____.
    a. the scientific method
    b. observation
    c. a worldview
    d. critical thinking skills

26. Benjamin Rush, the father of American psychiatry, advanced the moral therapy movement by
    _____.
    a. encouraging staff to treat patients with kindness and understanding
    b. signing the Patients' Bill of Rights
    c. discharging most of the patients in his care
    d. developing medications to treat psychosis

27. When designing her study on the effectiveness of drug treatment interventions, Dr. Spurrier took
    great care in obtaining a sample in such a way that each member of the population of interest had
    an equal probability of selection. Dr. Spurrier recognized the importance of a _____
    in research.
    a. naturalistic design
    b. random sample
    c. valid design
    d. dependent sample
    e. none of the above

28. While drawing conclusions from their findings, psychologists use statistical methods to determine
    the likelihood that differences between groups are _____ as opposed to chance
    fluctuations.
    a. manipulated
    b. significant
    c. reasonable
    d. important

29. Sarah has begun hearing voices that are not present. She has been referred to a psychologist to
    determine why she is experiencing these _____.
    a. delusions
    b. hallucinations
    c. humors
    d. melancholias

30. The interaction of genetic and environmental influences is represented by an individual's
    _____.
    a. genotype
    b. phenotype
    c. chromosomes
    d. predispositions

SHORT ANSWER
Answers are found at the end of this chapter. Answer the following short answer questions:

1. Discuss the criteria for determining whether behavior is abnormal.
2. Discuss the importance of considering sociocultural factors while assessing abnormality.
3. Discuss the policy of deinstitutionalization. What were the reasons for this policy? What are the criticisms of this policy?

4. Discuss the key features of critical thinking. Why are critical thinking skills important when reviewing information about abnormal psychology?
5. Explain why it is important not to infer causation from correlation.
6. Discuss the importance of the experimental method in scientific research. What variables are included in an experiment?
7. What is the biopsychosocial perspective? Explain its importance.
8. List and describe the four objectives of science.

ANSWERS TO MATCHING

1. moral therapy (p. 12)

2. psychologist (p. 3)

3. sample (p. 25)

4. catharsis (p. 16)

5. causal (p. 21)

6. correlation (p. 20)

7. significant (p. 19)

8. incidence (p. 25)

9. experimental subjects (p. 22)

10. description (p. 18)

11. blind (p. 22)

12. theory (p. 18)

13. positive correlation (p. 20)

14. longitudinal study (p. 21)

15. prevalence (p. 25)

16. dependent variable (p. 21)

17. construct validity (p. 24)

18. unobtrusive (p. 20)

19. psychodynamic model (p. 15)

20. scientific method (p. 19)

21. deinstitutionalization (p. 14)

22. medical model (p. 4)

23. psychological disorders (p. 3)

24. trephening (p. 9)

25. abnormal psychology (p. 4)

26. critical thinking (p. 30)

27. monozygotic twins (p. 26)

28. case study (p. 27)

29. dizygotic twins (p. 26)

30. informed consent (p. 20)

31. external validity (p. 24)

32. placebo (p. 23)

33. negative correlation (p. 20)

34. delusion (p. 7)

35. worldview (p. 9)

36. experimental method (p. 21)

37. independent variable (p. 21)

38. phenothiazines (p. 14)

39. hypnosis (p. 15)

40. internal validity (p. 24)

ANSWERS TO MULTIPLE CHOICE QUESTIONS

1. b. experimental (p. 21)

2. a. a reversal phase (p. 29)

3. b. prediction (p. 20)

4. b. population (p. 25)

5. b. public speaking performance is the dependent variable and modeling is the independent variable. (p. 21)

6. b. external validity. (p. 24)

7. c. negative (p. 20)

8. b. demonological (p. 9)

9. b. statistical analysis (p. 18)

10. d. a reversal design. (p. 27)

11. a. it provides considerable information about behavior, but cannot specify why a behavior occurs. (p. 20)

12. b. deinstitutionalization (p. 14)

13. a. phenothiazines (p. 14)

14. b. psychodynamic (p. 15)

15. b. scientific method (p. 19)

16. b. informed consent (p. 20)

17. b. experimental method (p. 21)

18. d. control subjects (p. 22)

19. b. double-blind placebo design (p. 23)

20. b. internal validity (p. 24)

21. b. epidemiological method (p. 25)

22. d. monozygotic (p. 26)

23. b. case study (p. 27)

24. a. the behavior improves whenever treatment is introduced, but returns to baseline levels during the reversal phase. (p. 27)

25. d. critical thinking skills (p. 30)

26. a. encouraging staff to treat patients with kindness and understanding (p. 12)

27. b. random sample (p. 25)

28. b. significant (p. 19)

29. b. hallucinations (p. 7)

30. b. phenotype (p. 27)

ANSWERS TO SHORT ANSWER QUESTIONS

1. Mental health professionals apply various criteria in making judgments about whether behavior is abnormal. The most commonly used criteria include whether the behavior exhibited is unusual, whether the behavior is socially unacceptable or violates social norms, if the individual's perception or interpretation of reality is faulty, if the person is in significant personal distress, if the exhibited behavior is maladaptive or self-defeating, and whether the behavior is dangerous. (pp. 5-7)

2. Behavior that is considered normal in one culture may be deemed abnormal in another. The description and expression of abnormal behavior may be significantly different from one culture to the next. As such, cultural context must not be ignored in the assessment of psychological disorders. (p. 8)

3. As a response to calls for reform in the early sixties, Congress established community mental health centers in an attempt to offer an alternative to long-term custodial care. Psychiatric patients were released from state mental hospitals under a policy of deinstitutionalization. Patients were often placed in less restrictive environments with the hope that they would achieve greater independence and self-sufficiency. Critics contend that the deinstitutionalization of patients has lead to their abandonment with few support systems in place to attend to their needs. (p. 14)

4. Critical thinking involves the adoption of a questioning attitude toward information one hears and reads. The key features of critical thinking include a skeptical attitude, evaluating the definition of terms, weighing assumptions on which statements are based, understanding that correlation is not causation, evaluating the evidence on which conclusions are based, avoiding oversimplification, and avoiding overgeneralization. (p. 30)

5. Correlational methods test the statistical relationship between variables. Correlations may allow for prediction but do not provide information regarding causation. Causal relationships may only be uncovered by the use of the experimental method. (p. 20)

6. The experimental method allows scientists to demonstrate cause-and-effect relationships between variables. The experimental method meets the scientific objective of explanation. The independent variable and dependent variable are included in experimental designs. The independent variable is the factor that is manipulated by the researcher. The dependent variable is the factor that is measured by the researcher. The independent variable is considered the cause; the dependent variable is considered the effect. (p. 21)

7. The biopsychosocial perspective is an interactionist model. According to this perspective, biological, psychological, and sociocultural factors must be considered when attempting to understand the development of psychological disorders. These factors provide a framework for intervention. (p. 17)

8. The four objectives of science include description, explanation, prediction, and control. Researchers attempt to meet these objectives through various research methodologies, including naturalistic observation (description), correlational studies (prediction), and experimental methods (explanation). (p. 18)

ANSWERS TO CROSSWORD

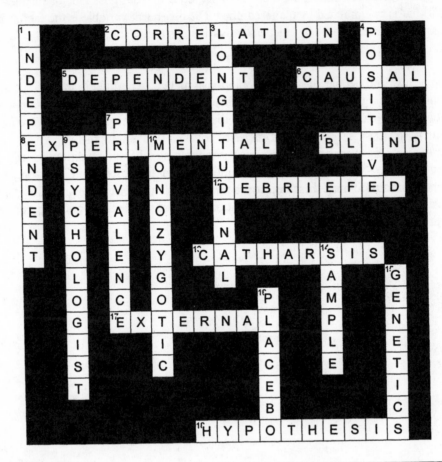

ACROSS

2. relationship between variables
5. variable that is measured in an experiment
6. cause and effect
8. method that aims to discover causal relationships
11. state of being unaware of whether one has received the experimental treatment
12. to be fully informed about an experiment after it has taken place
13. purgation of feelings
17. type of validity/degree to which experimental results can be generalized to other settings
18. an assumption that is tested through experimentation

DOWN

1. variable that is manipulated in an experiment
3. type of correlational study
4. type of correlation whereby increases in one variable are associated with increases in another
7. overall number of cases of a disorder
9. person with advanced graduate traing in psychology
10. twins that develop from the same fertilized egg
14. part of a population
15. science of heredity
16. an inert medication that is intended to control for expectancy effects

Chapter Two

Contemporary Perspectives on Abnormal Behavior

OBJECTIVES

1. Describe the various parts of the nervous system.
2. Discuss the lobes of the cerebral cortex by stating what functions each lobe controls.
3. Describe the psychodynamic model, including the structure of the mind, structure of the personality, defense mechanisms, and stages of psychosocial development.
4. Discuss the learning model's role of classical conditioning, operant conditioning, and social-cognitive theory.
5. Explain the humanistic model of abnormal behavior.
6. Compare and contrast the cognitive model's information-processing theory with the theories of Albert Ellis and Aaron Beck.
7. Explain the role of ethnicity on mental health.
8. Define the diathesis-stress model and describe how it impacts mental health.

CHAPTER OUTLINE

The Biological Perspective
    The Nervous System
    Evaluating Biological Perspectives on Abnormal Behavior
The Psychological Perspective
    Psychodynamic Models
    Learning Models
    Humanistic Models
    Cognitive Models
The Sociocultural Perspective
    Ethnicity and Mental Health
    Evaluating the Sociocultural Perspective
The Biopsychosocial Perspective
    The Diathesis-Stress Model
    Evaluating the Biopsychosocial Perspective
Summing Up

MATCHING

Answers are found at the end of this chapter.

Match these terms and concepts with the definitions that follow:

superego	repression
oral stage	ego
id	identification
defense mechanisms	soma
reinforcement	Oedipus complex
conditioned stimulus	synapse
central nervous system	neuron
positive reinforcement	negative reinforcement
diathesis	sympathetic division
reality principle	pleasure principle
archetypes	unconditioned stimulus
neurotransmitters	behavior modification
parasympathetic division	downward drift hypothesis
psychoanalytic theory	libido
magnification	self-actualization
object relations theory	punishment
serotonin	dopamine
hypothalamus	cerebral cortex
biopsychosocial perspective	cognitions
acetylcholine	denial

1. _____ governed by the reality principle, it is the psychic structure that corresponds to the concept of the self

2. _____ that which increases the likelihood of a response

3. _____ a type of cognitive error

4. _____ thoughts, beliefs, expectations, and attitudes

5. _____ primitive images that reside in the collective unconscious

6. _____ chemical substances that allow communication between neurons

7. _____ a nerve cell

8. _____ the theoretical model of personality developed by Freud

9. _____ sexual energy or drive

10. _____ the space between nerve cells

11. _____ a vulnerability to a stressor

12. _____ a psychosexual stage during which pleasure is sought through oral activities

13. _____ the brain and spinal cord

14. _____ becoming what you are capable of

15. _____ a neurotransmitter involved in regulation of mood

16. _____ part of the limbic system, it is involved in the regulation of body temperature, emotion, and motivation

17. _____ the application of learning principles in order to modify behavior

18. _____ stimuli that reduce the likelihood a behavior will be repeated

19. _____ a type of reinforcer that increases the frequency of a response

20. _____ the outer layer of the cerebrum associated with higher thought processes

21. _____ theory that links socioeconomic status and behavioral difficulty

22. _____ a psychodynamic theory that focuses upon the influence of internalized representations of attachment figures

23. _____ a type of neurotransmitter involved in Parkinson's disease

24. _____ the conflict which occurs during the phallic stage of development

25. _____ cell body

26. _____ paired with an unconditioned stimulus, it elicits a conditioned response

27. _____ the psychic structure governed by the pleasure principle

28. _____ a type of defense mechanism that involves the banishment of anxiety provoking ideas to the unconscious

29. _____ a division of the autonomic nervous system whose activity relaxes the body

30. _____ a model of abnormal behavior that focuses upon the interplay of sociocultural, biological, and psychological factors

31. _____ the process of incorporating the behaviors or personalities of others

32. _____ the psychic structure governed by the moral principle

33. _____ removal of an aversive stimulus that increases the frequency of a response

34. _____ a stimulus that triggers an unlearned response

35. _____ the governing principle of the ego

36. _____ psychological defenses preventing unacceptable impulses from rising into consciousness

37. _____ the governing principle of the id

38. _____ a division of the autonomic nervous system that arouses the body

39. _____ a type of neurotransmitter involved in Alzheimer's disease

40. _____ refusing to accept the true nature of a threat

CROSSWORD

Answers are found at the end of this chapter.

Complete the following crossword puzzle to reinforce your understanding of this chapter's key terms and concepts:

ACROSS		DOWN

ACROSS

1. a type of cognitive error
4. neurotransmitter involved in Alzheimer's disease
6. primitive images that reside in the collective unconscious
9. outer layer of the cerebrum associated with higher thought processes
12. theory developed by Freud
14. sexual energy or drive
15. reduces the likelihood a behavior will be repeated
16. space between neurons
17. refusing to accept the true nature of a threat
18. neurotransmitter involved in regulation of mood

DOWN

2. process of incorporating the behaviors and personalities of others
3. vulnerability to a stressor
5. brain and spinal cord
7. thoughts, beliefs, expectations
8. neurotransmitter involved in Parkinson's disease
10. governed by the reality principle
11. psychosexual stage during which pleasure in sought through oral activities
13. governed by the moral principle

MULTIPLE CHOICE

Answers are found at the end of this chapter.

The multiple choice questions listed will test your understanding of the material presented in the chapter.
Read through each question and circle the letter representing the best answer.

1. The _____ model seeks an understanding of abnormal behavior based upon the interplay of cultural, psychological, and biological factors.
    a. psychodynamic
    b. biopsychosocial
    c. interactionist
    d. diathesis-stress

2. _____ theorists focus upon the role of distorted thinking in the emergence of abnormal behavior.
    a. Cognitive
    b. Psychodynamic
    c. Biological
    d. Learning

3. The central nervous system consists of the _____.
    a. sympathetic and parasympathetic divisions
    b. brain and spinal cord
    c. frontal and occipital lobes
    d. autonomic and peripheral systems

4. Communication between neurons is _____ in nature.
    a. electrical
    b. chemical
    c. neuronal
    d. psychological

5. Sam has been diagnosed with clinical depression. His physician believes his depression is linked to dysfunctions involving _____.
    a. acetylcholine and dopamine
    b. dopamine
    c. serotonin and acetylcholine
    d. serotonin and norepinephrine

6. A tiny structure located between the thalamus and pituitary gland, the _____ is vital in regulating body temperature and motivation.
    a. reticular activating system
    b. hypothalamus
    c. cerebrum
    d. sympathetic nervous system

7. To Jung, the _____ represents the storehouse of archetypes or primitive images.
   a. id
   b. ego
   c. superego
   d. collective unconscious

8. Explanation of abnormal behavior in terms environmental factors such as rewards and punishments is characteristic of the _____ model.
   a. psychodynamic
   b. cognitive
   c. correlational
   d. learning

9. In Pavlov's experiment, the food was the _____.
   a. conditioned stimulus
   b. unconditioned stimulus
   c. conditioned response
   d. unconditioned response

10. Salivation as the result of the presentation of food is known as a _____.
    a. conditioned stimulus
    b. unconditioned response
    c. conditioned response
    d. unconditioned stimulus

11. Which is true of behavior modification?
    a. It provides considerable information about behavior but cannot specify why a behavior occurs.
    b. It involves the systematic application of learning principles to alter behavior.
    c. It frequently employs biological interventions to modify problem behaviors.
    d. It is of little value for studying abnormal behavior.

12. After a break up with her partner, Alexandra said she didn't think anyone would ever ask her out again. Alexandra's belief is an example of _____.
    a. selective abstraction
    b. overgeneralization
    c. conditional regard
    d. a conditioned response

13. Social-cognitive theorists emphasize the role of observational learning, or _____, in human behavior.
    a. classical conditioning
    b. self-actualization
    c. cognitive distortions
    d. modeling

14. The _____ model provided the first psychological perspective on abnormal behavior.
    a. biopsychsocial
    b. psychodynamic
    c. medical
    d. psychosomatic

15. Overutilization of the neurotransmitter _____ may account for the development of schizophrenia.
    a. acetylcholine
    b. serotonin
    c. norephinephrine
    d. dopamine

16. According to psychodynamic theorists, structures of personality include the _____.
    a. unconscious, preconscious, and subconscious
    b. id, ego, and superego
    c. oral, anal, phallic, latent, and genital
    d. pleasure, reality, and moral

17. Sam avoids giving a speech that has caused him great anxiety in preparing for. Through avoidance, he has reduced his anxiety and is now more likely to avoid similar speeches in the future. From a learning perspective, this type of avoidance is an example of _____.
    a. positive reinforcement
    b. negative reinforcement
    c. punishment
    d. behavior modification

18. Many cognitive psychologists are influenced by the concepts of _____.
    a. the unconscious
    b. computer science
    c. humanism
    d. psychosexual development

19. All of the following are associated with cognitive theory, except
    a. A-B-C approach.
    b. cognitive distortions.
    c. individual psychology.
    d. rational emotive therapy.

20. The nervous system is made up of billions of nerve cells called _____.
    a. dendrites
    b. neurotransmitters
    c. soma
    d. neurons

21. The diathesis-stress model of genetic-environmental interaction suggests that
    a. biological vulnerability combined with environmental stress results in abnormal behavior.
    b. phenotypic vulnerability combined with inappropriate learning results in abnormal behavior.
    c. prenatal stress combined with environmental stress results in abnormal behavior.
    d. biological vulnerability produces stress, which results in abnormal behavior.

22. According to Freud, excessive self-control and perfectionism may begin at the _____ stage of psychosexual development.
    a. oral
    b. anal
    c. genital
    d. latency

23. _____ theorists believe it is important to understand the obstacles that people encounter as they strive toward self-actualization and authenticity.
    a. Cognitive
    b. Humanistic
    c. Behavioral
    d. Psychodynamic

24. _____ decreases the likelihood that a behavior will repeat.
    a. Reinforcement
    b. Negative reinforcement
    c. Avoidance
    d. Punishment

25. Both negative reinforcement and punishment involve negative stimuli that decrease or suppress the frequency of a behavior.
    a. True
    b. False

26. Food, water, sexual stimulation, and escape from pain are all considered _____.
    a. meta-needs
    b. primary reinforcers
    c. secondary reinforcers
    d. expectancies

27. Ellis' cognitive model utilizes an A-B-C approach to explain the causes of negative emotions. In this model, therapists focus upon _____.
    a. antecedents, behaviors, and consequences
    b. activating events, beliefs, and consequences
    c. activating events, behaviors, and causes
    d. antecedents, beliefs, and causes

28. According to Aaron Beck, selective abstraction, overgeneralization, and magnification are examples of _____, which lead to emotional distress.
   a. cognitive errors
   b. meta-needs
   c. expectancies
   d. delusions

29. Keri has forgotten that a difficult paper is due. According to Freud, which defense mechanism is at work?
   a. repression
   b. regression
   c. projection
   d. rationalization

30. The autonomic nervous system regulates all of the following activities, except
   a. heart rate.
   b. respiration.
   c. digestion.
   d. walking.

SHORT ANSWER
Answers are found at the end of this chapter. Answer the following short answer questions:

1. Discuss the diathesis-stress model. How does it represent an interactionist approach to explaining abnormal behavior?
2. Discuss the importance of neurotransmission.
3. From a learning perspective, discuss how a fear or phobia may be developed.
4. Explain the downward drift hypothesis.
5. How may abnormal behavior be understood from a cognitive perspective?

ANSWERS TO MATCHING

1. ego (p. 39)

2. reinforcement (p. 50)

3. magnification (p. 56)

4. cognitions (p. 54)

5. archetypes (p. 44)

6. neurotransmitters (p. 34)

7. neuron (p. 33)

8. psychoanalytic theory (p. 38)

9. libido (p. 41)

10. synapse (p. 34)

11. diathesis (p. 60)

12. oral stage (p. 41)

13. central nervous system (p. 35)

14. self-actualization (p. 53)

15. serotonin (p. 35)

16. hypothalamus (p. 36)

17. behavior modification (p. 52)

18. punishment (p. 50)

19. positive reinforcement (p. 50)

20. cerebral cortex (p. 37)

21. downward drift hypothesis (p. 59)

22. object relations theory (p. 45)

23. dopamine (p. 35)

24. Oedipus complex (p. 42)

25. soma (p. 33)

26. conditioned stimulus (p. 49)

27. id (p. 39)

28. repression (p. 40)

29. parasympathetic division (p. 37)

30. biopsychosocial perspective (p. 60)

31. identification (p. 40)

32. superego (p. 40)

33. negative reinforcement (p. 50)

34. unconditioned stimulus (p. 49)

35. reality principle (p. 39)

36. defense mechanisms (p. 40)

37. pleasure principle (p. 39)

38. sympathetic division (p. 37)

39. acetylcholine (p. 3)

40. denial (p. 40)

ANSWERS TO MULTIPLE CHOICE QUESTIONS

1. b. biopsychosocial (p. 60)

2. a. Cognitive (p. 54)

3. b. brain and spinal cord (p. 35)

4. b. chemical (p. 34)

5. d. serotonin and norepinephrine (p. 35)

6. b. hypothalamus (p. 36)

7. d. collective unconscious (p. 44)

8. d. learning (pp. 47, 50)

9. b. unconditioned stimulus (p. 49)

10. b. unconditioned response (p. 49)

11. b. It involves the systematic application of learning principles to alter behavior. (p. 52)

12. b. overgeneralization (p. 56)

13. d. modeling (p. 51)

14. b. psychodynamic (p. 38)

15. d. dopamine (p. 35)

16. b. id, ego, and superego (p. 39)

17. b. negative reinforcement (p. 50)

18. b. computer science (p. 54)

19. c. individual psychology. (p. 44)

20. d. neurons (p. 33)

21. a. biological vulnerability combined with environmental stress results in abnormal behavior. (p. 60)

22. b. anal (p. 42)

23. b. Humanistic (p. 53)

24. d. Punishment (p. 50)

25. b. False (p. 50)

26. b. primary reinforcers (p. 50)

27. b. activating events, beliefs, and consequences (p. 55)

28. a. cognitive errors (p. 54)

29. a. repression (p. 40)

30. d. walking (p. 37)

ANSWERS TO SHORT ANSWER QUESTIONS

1. The diathesis-stress model is an interactionist model. Abnormal behaviors are viewed as a consequence of biopsychosocial variables. A diathesis, or genetic vulnerability, may interact with an environmental stress to bring about the development of a disorder. Environmental stressors may include trauma, sexual or physical abuse, family conflict, or other significant life circumstances or changes. The stronger the vulnerability, the less environmental stress is needed to produce a disorder. (p. 60)

2. Neurotransmission refers to the chemical communication between nerve cells at the synaptic level. Irregularities at this level are correlated with abnormal behavior patterns. Irregularities in the transmission of serotonin are linked to depression and eating disorders. Irregularities in dopamine transmission may be involved in the development of schizophrenia. Thoughts and mental images are related to the functioning of these and other neurotransmitters in the brain. As such, neurotransmission is significantly related to an individual's behavior and mental process. (pp. 34,35)

3. Fears and phobias may be understood within a behavioral framework, specifically a classical conditioning framework. According to learning theorists, individuals often learn by association. Individuals may associate what was once a neutral stimulus with a stimulus which is aversive or threatening. For example, an individual may associate a dog (once a neutral stimulus for the person) with a traumatic event (being bitten). Conditioning (learning) follows from association. As such, the person may be conditioned to fear dogs. Following the trauma, exposure to any dog may elicit or trigger a fear response. (p. 51)

4. The downward drift hypothesis suggests there is a correlation between low socioeconomic status and abnormal behavior patterns. The hypothesis suggests that abnormal behavior patterns lead individuals to drift downward in socioeconomic status. If an individual suffers from an addiction, for example, he/she is likely to lose social status and drift downward economically. (p. 59)

5. According to cognitive theorists, it is the perception of events, not the events themselves, which determines one's emotional state. Distortions in the perception of events may lead to psychological disorders. For example, a depressed person may have a pessimistic view of the world or magnify the significance of negative events. According to Beck, emotional distress is often the consequence of four basic types of cognitive errors. These include selective abstraction, overgeneralization, magnification, and absolutist thinking. These irrational cognitive patterns foster negative emotions and oftentimes abnormal behavior. (pp. 54,56)

ANSWERS TO CROSSWORD

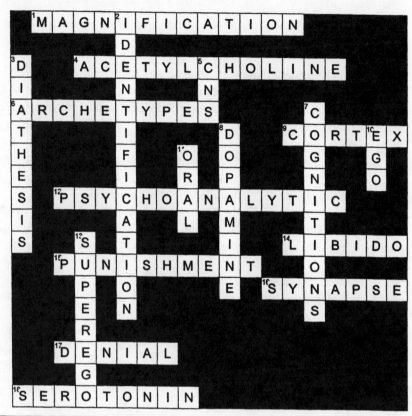

ACROSS		DOWN
1. a type of cognitive error	16. space between neurons	2. process of incorporating the behaviors and personalities of others
4. neurotransmitter involved in Alzheimer's disease	17. refusing to accept the true nature of a threat	3. vulnerability to a stressor
6. primitive images that reside in the collective unconscious	18. neurotransmitter involved in regulation of mood	5. brain and spinal cord
9. outer layer of the cerebrum associated with higher thought processes		7. thoughts, beliefs, expectations
12. theory developed by Freud		8. neurotransmitter involved in Parkinson's disease
14. sexual energy or drive		10. governed by the reality principle
15. reduces the likelihood a behavior will be repeated		11. psychosexual stage during which pleasure in sought through oral activities
		13. governed by the moral principle

Chapter Three

Classification and Assessment of Abnormal Behavior

OBJECTIVES

1. Discuss historical origins of modern diagnostic systems and the development of the DSM system.
2. Describe the features of the DSM system and evaluate its strengths and weaknesses.
3. Discuss the role of sociocultural and ethnic factors in the classification of abnormal behavior.
4. Describe approaches used by investigators to demonstrate the reliability and validity of methods of assessment.
5. Describe the features of the mental status examination and different types of interviewing techniques.
6. Describe the features of tests of intelligence and personality.
7. Describe the use of psychological tests in the assessment of neuropsychological functioning.
8. Discuss the advantages and limitations of behavioral assessment, and describe the following behavioral techniques: the behavioral interview, self-monitoring, use of analogue measures, and behavioral rating scales.
9. Discuss cognitive measures of assessment.
10. Discuss the use of physiological measures in assessment, including the use of brain-imaging techniques.

CHAPTER OUTLINE
Classification of Abnormal Behavior
       The DSM and Models of Abnormal Behavior
Issues of Reliability and Validity in Assessment
       Reliability
       Validity
       Sociocultural and Ethnic Factors in the Assessment of Abnormal Behavior
Methods of Assessment
       The Clinical Interview
       Psychological Tests
       Neuropsychological Assessment
       Behavioral Assessment
       Cognitive Assessment
       Physiological Measurement
Summing Up

MATCHING

Answers are found at the end of this chapter. Match these terms and concepts with the definitions that follow:

reactivity	PET scan
mental status exam	EEG
reliable	validity
predictive validity	analogue measure
construct validity	concurrent validity
functional analysis	CT scan
projective tests	objective tests
IQ	mental age
self-monitoring	galvanic skin response
MRI	DSM
syndrome	hypothyroidism
culture-bound syndrome	sanism
internal consistency	clinical interview
temporal stability	false negative
specificity	phrenology
structured interview	unstructured interview
CASPER	reality testing
TAT	neuropsychological assessment
psychometric approach	behavioral rating scale
Automatic Thoughts Questionnaire	BEAM

1. _____ a sophisticated type of EEG that analyzes brain wave patterns and reveals areas of activity from moment to moment

2. _____ that which is consistent

3. _____ the degree to which a test score is predictive of some future behavior

4. _____ intended to simulate the setting in which a behavior naturally occurs

5. _____ an imaging technique that monitors glucose utilization within the brain

6. _____ a behavioral analysis that examines the antecedents and consequences of behavior

7. _____ a measure of intelligence

8. _____ observing one's own behavior, emotions, or thoughts

9. _____ an image of the brain formed by measuring the signals emitted when the head is placed in a strong magnetic field

10. _____ a disorder found within only a few cultural contexts

33

11. _____ psychological tests that present ambiguous stimuli onto which an individual is thought to project his or her personality or unconscious motives

12. _____ the tendency for observed behavior to be influenced by the manner in which it is measured

13. _____ a structured clinical assessment to determine various aspects of the client's mental functioning

14. _____ a classification system for the diagnosis of mental disorders

15. _____ the negative stereotyping of individuals who are identified as mentally ill

16. _____ the degree to which a test measures the hypothetical construct that it claims to measure

17. _____ tests that allow a limited range of response options which may be scored objectively

18. _____ identifying an individual as not having a disorder who truly has a disorder

19. _____ a type of interview whereby the clinician adopts his or her own style of questioning without following a standard format

20. _____ a computerized interview system

21. _____ a cluster of symptoms characteristic of a particular disease

22. _____ caused by a deficiency of thyroxin and characterized by lethargy

23. _____ interrelationships of items on a test

24. _____ consistency of test responses over time

25. _____ the degree to which test responses predict scores on criterion measures taken at about the same time

26. _____ determining personality by examining bumps on an individual's head

27. _____ an interview that follows a preset format

28. _____ the age equivalent that corresponds to an individual's level of intelligence as measured by the Stanford-Binet Intelligence Scale

29. _____ a projective test that consists of a series of cards, each of which depicts an ambiguous scene

34

30. _____ used to evaluate whether psychological problems reflect underlying neurological damage

31. _____ an assessment method that relies on psychological tests to identify and measure traits which compose an individual's personality

32. _____ a checklist used to record the frequency of occurrence of a target behavior

33. _____ a measure of the change in electrical activity of the skin

34. _____ measures the electrical activity of the brain

35. _____ an X-ray of the brain that provides information regarding its internal structures

36. _____ the degree to which a test measures what it purports to measure

37. _____ the ability to perceive the world accurately

38. _____ a cognitive assessment whereby clients rate the frequency and degree of conviction associated with thirty automatic negative thoughts

39. _____ the ability of a test to avoid classifying individuals as having a disorder when they do not have the disorder

40. _____ the most widely used means of assessment

CROSSWORD

Answers are found at the end of this chapter. Complete the following crossword puzzle to reinforce your understanding of this chapter's key terms and concepts:

ACROSS

2. observing one's own behavior, emotions, or thoughts
7. a measure of intelligence
9. measures the electrical activity of the brain
11. disorder found within only a few cultural contexts
13. a computerized interview system
14. the tendency for observed behavior to be influenced by the manner in which it is measured
15. that which is consistent

DOWN

1. intended to simulate the setting in which a behavior occurs naturally
2. the negative stereotyping of individuals who are identified as mentally ill
3. identifying an individual as not having a disorder who truly has a disorder
4. an x-ray of the brain that provides information regarding its internal structures
5. an interview that follows a preset format
6. the degree to which a test measures what it purports to measure
8. psychological tests that present ambiguous stimuli
10. an imaging technique that monitors glucose utilization
12. a classification system for the diagnosis of mental disorders

MULTIPLE CHOICE

Answers are found at the end of this chapter. The multiple choice questions listed will test your understanding of the material presented in the chapter. Read through each question and circle the letter representing the best answer.

1. Criterion validity has two general types. These include
   a. content and concurrent .
   b. construct and content.
   c. construct and predictive.
   d. concurrent and predictive.

2. Specific diagnostic criteria in DSM-IV _____.
   a. include essential features and associated features
   b. group behaviors according to their underlying causes
   c. are grouped according to psychodynamic theory
   d. are explanatory

3. Which brain-imaging technique requires an individual to be placed in a tunnel that generates a strong magnetic field?
   a. MRI
   b. PET
   c. CT Scan
   d. BEAM

4. The major value of the structured interview is in _____.
   a. its ability to produce high reliability without special training of interviewers
   b. minimizing interviewing time
   c. validity of diagnosis
   d. reliability of diagnostic classification

5. The Automatic Thoughts Questionnaire is an example of _____.
   a. a cognitive assessment measure
   b. a behavioral assessment measure
   c. a personality assessment measure
   d. a psychodynamic assessment measure

6. The DSM classification system is an outgrowth of the work of _____.
   a. Hippocrates
   b. Kraeplin
   c. Freud
   d. Murray

7. Questions in the MMPI-2 _____.
   a. are open ended
   b. were selected because they discriminated between normal and clinical diagnostic populations
   c. were chosen because they have a single correct answer
   d. were chosen to detect individuals trying to "fake good"

8. The degree to which a test correctly identifies people who have a particular disorder is referred to as _____.
   a. sensitivity
   b. specificity
   c. face validity
   d. concurrent reliability

9. An advantage of the Wechsler intelligence scales is
   a. relative strengths and weaknesses of an individual are assessed.
   b. an examiner is not necessary.
   c. questions are age graded.
   d. an individual's mental age can be determined.

10. A clinician who asks a series of questions about problem behavior, their histories, and their relationships to situational events is using which method of assessment?
   a. the behavioral interview
   b. the mental status examination
   c. self-monitoring
   d. a projective assessment

11. The _____ is a projective test that requires individuals to respond to an ambiguous scene by constructing a story.
   a. MMPI-2
   b. TAT
   c. BDI
   d. MCMI

12. All of the following are clinical scales on the MMPI-2, except
   a. Masculinity-Femininity
   b. Depression
   c. Psychasthenia
   d. Mania

13. The Stanford-Binet and the Wechsler Scales are used to measure _____.
   a. behavioral responses
   b. intelligence
   c. mood
   d. cognitions

14. Which of the following is not true of computerized clinical interviews?
    a. Computerized interviews are actually more time consuming for clinicians because the clinician needs to review the client's answers and take time to ask the client questions that the computer is not programmed to ask.
    b. Computers can be programmed to ask questions in a specific order.
    c. The client may be less embarrassed about sharing information with a computer than with a clinician.
    d. Clients tend to report a greater number of problems to the computer than to clinicians.

15. All of the following are subtests on the Halstead-Reitan Neuropsychological Battery, except
    a. the Visual-Auditory test.
    b. the Rhythm test.
    c. the Category test.
    d. the Tactual Performance test.

16. The disadvantage of self-rating scales is that _____.
    a. they are costly to administer
    b. many clients find them difficult to complete
    c. good interrater reliability is difficult to achieve
    d. test responses may be biased

17. Which of the following would be coded on Axis IV of the DSM-IV?
    a. a personality disorder
    b. a medical disorder
    c. the clinician's opinion of the client's overall level of functioning
    d. problems in the social or physical environment that affect the diagnosis, treatment, and outcome of psychological disorders

18. The MMPI-2 is to _____ as the MCMI is to _____.
    a. abnormal behavior patterns; personality style
    b. personality style; abnormal behavior patterns
    c. essential features; associated features
    d. associated features; essential features

19. An example of a culture-bound syndrome is _____.
    a. mental retardation
    b. depression
    c. schizophrenia
    d. anorexia nervosa

20. An electromyograph measures _____.
    a. brain waves
    b. muscle tension
    c. neurotransmission
    d. soft tissue

21. Which type of validity refers to the degree to which test items bear an apparent relationship to the constructs they purport to measure?
    a. face validity
    b. criterion validity
    c. predictive validity
    d. concurrent validity

22. All of the following are included in a mental status exam, except
    a. behavioral observations.
    b. appearance.
    c. thinking processes.
    d. rapport.

23. Which of the following is the most widely used means of assessment and is employed by essentially all helping professionals?
    a. the MMPI-2
    b. the Rorschach
    c. the MCMI
    d. the clinical interview

24. Which of the following is a major advantage of the DSM-IV?
    a. it eliminates multiple diagnoses
    b. high validity
    c. high reliability
    d. it develops a comprehensive view as a result of its multiaxial system

25. From which of the following theoretical perspectives might an interviewer try to focus on antecedents or stimulus cues related to a specific event?
    a. psychodynamic
    b. behavioral
    c. cognitive
    d. humanistic

26. According to the DSM-IV, a mental disorder requires _____.
    a. a behavior pattern that does not represent an expected or culturally appropriate response to a stressful event.
    b. statistically uncommon behavior.
    c. the demonstration of a biological cause.
    d. an expected response to a stressful situation.

27. Housing and economic problems affecting the diagnosis, treatment, and outcome of a psychological disorder are listed under _____ of the DSM-IV.
    a. Axis I
    b. Axis II
    c. Axis III
    d. Axis IV
    e. Axis V

28. Examination of behavior in terms of antecedent stimuli and reinforcement consequence is known as a _____.
    a. clinical assessment
    b. functional analysis
    c. psychometric assessment
    d. cognitive assessment

29. During the clinical interview, most clinicians obtain information regarding
    a. the psychosocial history of the client.
    b. a description of the presenting problem.
    c. medical history.
    d. all of the above.

30. Questions from the Mental Status Examination such as "Would you please tell me your name," and "Do you know what the date is today" help assess _____.
    a. orientation
    b. mood
    c. insight
    d. judgment

SHORT ANSWER
Answers are found at the end of this chapter. Answer the following short answer questions:

1. Discuss the features of the Diagnostic and Statistical Manual of Mental Disorders (DSM).
2. How is the DSM evaluated?
3. Discuss the various types of validity as they pertain to assessment measures.
4. Discuss the role of neuropsychological assessments in the evaluation of psychological problems.
5. Discuss the methods used in the cognitive assessment of those with psychological problems.

VIDEO/CD-ROM
In order to obtain greater insight into the information presented in this chapter, refer to the video that accompanies it.

Video 3.1   Administration of Projective Tests: Dr. Ruth Monroe

ANSWERS TO MATCHING

1. BEAM (p. 94)

2. reliable (p. 68)

3. predictive validity (p. 68)

4. analogue measure (p. 90)

5. PET scan (p. 93)

6. functional analysis (p. 87)

7. IQ (p. 78)

8. self-monitoring (p. 89)

9. MRI (p. 93)

10. culture-bound syndrome (p. 67)

11. projective tests (p. 83)

12. reactivity (p. 88)

13. mental status exam (p. 75)

14. DSM (p. 63)

15. sanism (p. 70)

16. construct validity (p. 72)

17. objective tests (p. 80)

18. false negative (p. 72)

19. unstructured interview (p. 75)

20. CASPER (p. 76)

21. syndrome (p. 65)

22. hypothyroidism (p. 66)

23. internal consistency (p. 71)

24. temporal stability (p. 71)

25. concurrent validity (p. 72)

26. phrenology (p. 73)

27. structured interview (p. 75)

28. mental age (p. 77)

29. TAT (p. 84)

30. neuropsychological assessment (p. 85)

31. psychometric approach (p. 87)

32. behavioral rating scale (p. 90)

33. galvanic skin response (p. 92)

34. EEG (p. 92)

35. CT scan (p. 92)

36. validity (p. 68)

37. reality testing (p. 84)

38. Automatic Thoughts Questionnaire (p. 91)

39. specificity (p. 72)

40. clinical interview (p. 74)

ANSWERS TO MULTIPLE CHOICE QUESTIONS

1. d. concurrent and predictive. (p. 72)

2. a. include essential features and associated features (p. 64)

3. a. MRI (p. 93)

4. d. reliability of diagnostic classification (p. 75)

5. a. a cognitive assessment measure (p. 91)

6. b. Kraeplin (p. 63)

7. b. were selected because they discriminated between normal and clinical diagnostic populations (p. 80)

8. a. sensitivity (p. 72)

9. a. relative strengths and weaknesses of an individual are assessed. (p. 78)

10. a. the behavioral interview (p. 87)

11. b. TAT (p. 84)

12. d. mania (p. 81)

13. b. intelligence (p. 77)

14. a. Computerized interviews are actually more time consuming for clinicians because the clinician needs to review the client's answers and take time to ask the client questions that the computer is not programmed to ask. (p. 76)

15. a. the Visual-Auditory test. (p. 86)

16. d. test responses may be biased (p. 82)

17. d. problems in the social or physical environment that affect the diagnosis, treatment, and outcome of psychological disorders (p. 65)

18. a. abnormal behavior patterns; personality style (p. 82)

19. d. anorexia nervosa (p. 68)

20. b. muscle tension (p. 92)

21. a. face validity (p. 72)

22. d. rapport. (p. 75)

23. d. the clinical interview (p. 74)

24. d. it develops a comprehensive view as a result of its multiaxial system (p. 70)

25. b. behavioral (p. 87)

26. a. behavior pattern that does not represent an expected or culturally appropriate response to a stressful event. (p. 63)

27. d. Axis IV (p. 66)

28. b. functional analysis (p. 87)

29. d. all of the above. (p. 74)

30. a. orientation (p. 75)

ANSWERS TO SHORT ANSWER QUESTIONS

1. The Diagnostic and Statistical Manual of Mental Disorders (DSM) is a classification system that describes the diagnostic features of abnormal behaviors. The DSM does not explain the cause of abnormal behaviors. The DSM has three features. These include the utilization of specific diagnostic criteria, the grouping of abnormal behavior patterns that share clinical features, and a multiaxial system. (pp. 64, 65)

2. Reliability and validity are used as criteria for evaluating the DSM. Reliability, or consistency, refers to whether those making diagnoses are likely to arrive at the same diagnosis when evaluating the same cases. Validity is tested by examining whether those who receive a particular diagnosis exhibit behaviors in keeping with those represented by the diagnostic category. The DSM's predictive validity is based upon its ability to predict the course of a disorder or response to treatment. Research supports the reliability and validity of many of the DSM's diagnostic classes, such as mood and anxiety disorders. The reliability and validity of other diagnostic categories, such as the personality disorders, remain unclear and at times controversial. (p. 68)

3. Assessment measures are evaluated by their ability to measure what they are intended to measure. This is known as a test's validity. Validity is measured by means of content, criterion, and construct validity. The degree to which the content of an assessment tool covers a representative sample of the content it is supposed to measure is referred to as content validity. Tools assessing anxiety should have items addressing features of anxiety. Criterion validity includes both concurrent and predictive measures. Concurrent validity refers to the degree to which responses predict scores on standard measures taken at approximately the same time, whereas predictive validity refers to a test's ability to predict future behaviors. Finally, construct validity refers to the degree to which an assessment measure corresponds to the underlying construct it is supposed to measure. (p. 72)

4. Neuropsychological assessments are utilized to determine the existence of underlying neurological problems as they relate to abnormal behaviors. Brain imaging techniques, in addition to behavioral observation and psychological testing may reveal the presence of brain damage and the location of this damage. (p. 85)

5. According to cognitive theorists, abnormal behavior is often the result of distortions in thinking patterns. There are several methods used in the cognitive assessment of those with psychological disorders. These include the use of thought records or diaries, whereby the client reports thought patterns connected with upsetting emotional states. Inventories such as the Automatic Thoughts Questionnaire and Dysfunctional Attitudes Scale are also used. Clients rate the frequency and degree to which they agree with attitudes and thoughts related to depression and anxiety. (pp. 90, 92)

ANSWERS TO CROSSWORD

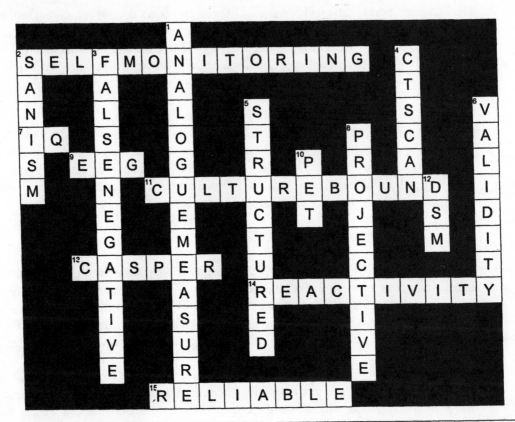

ACROSS

2. observing one's own behavior, emotions, or thoughts
7. a measure of intelligence
9. measures the electrical activity of the brain
11. disorder found within only a few cultural contexts
13. a computerized interview system
14. the tendency for observed behavior to be influenced by the manner in which it is measured
15. that which is consistent

DOWN

1. intended to simulate the setting in which a behavior occurs naturally
2. the negative stereotyping of individuals who are identified as mentally ill
3. identifying an individual as not having a disorder who truly has a disorder
4. an x-ray of the brain that provides information regarding its internal structures
5. an interview that follows a preset format
6. the degree to which a test measures what it purports to measure
8. psychological tests that present ambiguous stimuli
10. an imaging technique that monitors glucose utilization
12. a classification system for the diagnosis of mental disorders

Chapter Four

Methods of Treatment

OBJECTIVES

1. Describe the different types of mental health professionals and the basic features of psychotherapy.
2. Describe the goals and methods of traditional psychoanalysis and compare and contrast traditional psychoanalysis with modern psychodynamic approaches.
3. Describe the goals and methods of behavioral therapy.
4. Describe the goals and methods of humanistic therapies.
5. Describe the goals and methods of cognitive therapy.
6. Discuss the development of eclectic approaches in psychotherapy.
7. Describe the features and roles of group therapy and marital and family therapy.
8. Summarize the findings of research into the effectiveness of psychotherapy in general and specific therapeutic techniques in particular.
9. Discuss issues relating to the use of traditional Western psychotherapy approaches with diverse cultural and racial groups.
10. Discuss the various drug therapies, including antianxiety drugs, antipsychotic drugs, antidepressants, and lithium.
11. Describe the other biomedical treatments, including electroconvulsive therapy and psychosurgery.
12. Describe the contemporary roles of the community mental health center and the mental hospital and the problems of the psychiatric homeless population.

CHAPTER OUTLINE

Types of Mental Health Professionals
Psychotherapy
       Psychodynamic Therapy
       Behavior Therapy
       Humanistic Therapy
       Cognitive Therapy
       Cognitive-Behavioral Therapy
       Eclectic Therapy
       Group, Family, and Marital Therapy
       Evaluating Methods of Treatment
       Multicultural Issues in Psychotherapy
Biomedical Therapies
       Drug Therapy
       Ethnic Differences in Response to Psychotropic medication
       Electroconvulsive Therapy
       Psychosurgery
       Evaluation of Biological Approaches
Hospitalization and Community-Based Care
       Roles for Hospitalization
       The Community Mental Health Center
       Ethnic Group Differences in Use of Mental Health Services

Racial Stereotyping and the Mental Health System
Evaluation of Deinstitutionalization
Summing Up

MATCHING

Answers are found at the end of this chapter. Match these terms and concepts with the definitions that follow:

nonspecific factors	transference relationship
psychotherapy	empathy
latent content	manifest content
systematic desensitization	token economy
person-centered therapy	unconditional positive regard
REBT	cognitive distortions
family therapy	meta-analysis
ECT	deinstitutionalization
primary prevention	secondary prevention
tricyclics	SSRIs
tolerance	rebound anxiety
neuroleptics	psychopharmacology
managed care systems	CBT
congruence	genuineness
modeling	countertransference
insight	resistance
free association	psychoanalysis
eclectic orientation	displacing
object relations	client-centered therapy
antidepressants	lithium

1. _____ a structured form of treatment consisting of one or more verbal interactions between client and therapist

2. _____ a therapeutic approach that focuses on replacing irrational, maladaptive beliefs with more adaptive beliefs

3. _____ errors in thinking

4. _____ HMOs

5. _____ the study of psychiatric medications and their effects

6. _____ common features of psychotherapy that are not specific to any one form of therapy

7. _____ the material of a dream the individual experiences and reports

8. _____ strong anxiety following withdrawal from an antianxiety medication

9. _____ antidepressant medications that block the reuptake or reabsorbtion of serotonin

10. _____ the policy of reintegrating mental patients into society

11. _____ a behavioral technique involving the exposure to progressively more fearful stimuli while remaining relaxed. Used for the treatment of phobias

12. _____ incorporating psychodynamic, behavioral, humanistic, and cognitive approaches

13. _____ therapy in which the family, not the individual, is the focus of treatment

14. _____ a technique involving the administration of electrical shock to the head

15. _____ a group of antidepressant medications that increase the activity of norepinephrine and serotonin in the brain

16. _____ preventing problems from arising in the first place

17. _____ a medication that stabilizes the mood swings of patients with bipolar disorder

18. _____ transferring impulses toward unacceptable objects onto more acceptable objects

19. _____ the transfer of feelings that the therapist holds toward others persons onto a client

20. _____ the symbolic content of a dream

21. _____ learning desired behaviors through the observation of others

22. _____ also called person-centered therapy

23. _____ unconditionally accepting

24. _____ a therapy that focuses on changing overt behavior and underlying thoughts

25. _____ a physiological sign of dependence

26. _____ medications used to treat depression

27. _____ a method of psychotherapy developed by Freud

28. _____ the blocking of thoughts or emotions that would elicit anxiety

29. _____ an operant conditioning technique in which clients earn tokens for performing appropriate behaviors

30. _____ understanding someone's experiences from their point of view

31. _____ a statistical technique averaging the results of large numbers of studies

32. _____ a type of humanistic therapy characterized by acceptance

33. _____ the client's transfer of emotions or attitudes onto the therapist

34. _____ attempts to reduce existing problems at an early stage

35. _____ antipsychotic drugs

36. _____ verbalizing uncensored thoughts as they come to mind

37. _____ the individual's relationships to the internalized representations of others' personalities that have been introjected within the individual's ego structure

38. _____ the ability to be open about one's feelings

39. _____ the fit between one's thoughts, emotions, and behavior

40. _____ awareness and understanding of one's motives and emotions

CROSSWORD

Answers are found at the end of this chapter. Complete the following crossword puzzle to reinforce your understanding of this chapter's key terms and concepts:

ACROSS	DOWN

ACROSS

3. structured treatment consisting of one or more client therapist interactions
4. therapy that focuses on overt behavior and underlying thoughts
8. strong anxiety following withdrawal from antianxiety medication
9. humanistic therapy
10. stabilizes the mood swings of clients with bipolar disorder
12. incorporating several therapeutic approaches
13. antidepressants that block the reuptake of serotonin
14. awareness of one's motives and emotions
16. learning behavior through the observation of others

DOWN

1. a technique involving the administration of electrical shock to the head
2. antipsychotic drugs
3. method of psychotherapy developed by Freud
5. a physiological sign of dependence
6. antidepressant medications that increase the activity of norepinephrine and serotonin
7. understanding someone's experiences from his or her point of view
11. a therapeutic approach that focuses on replacing irrational thoughts with adaptive ones
15. managed care systems

MULTIPLE CHOICE

Answers are found at the end of this chapter.

The multiple choice questions listed will test your understanding of the material presented in the chapter.
Read through each question and circle the letter representing the best answer.

1. Which of the following is the process of uttering uncensored thoughts as they come to mind?
    a. free association
    b. insight
    c. rational emotive speech
    d. cognitive interpretation

2. Which of the following is not one of the defining characteristics of psychotherapy?
    a. The process of psychotherapy involves systematic interactions between clients and therapists.
    b. Psychotherapists draw upon psychological principles, research, and theory in their practice.
    c. Psychotherapy may be directed at behavioral, cognitive, and emotional domains to help clients overcome psychological difficulties.
    d. Psychotherapy involves a core fundamental system of interaction and techniques used by all therapeutic orientations.

3. A psychotherapist having difficulties in his marriage begins arguing more and more with his female clients. His behavior may be an illustration of
    a. transference.
    b. latent content.
    c. manifest content.
    d. countertransference.

4. All of the following are antidepressant medications, except
    a. fluoxetine (Prozac).
    b. sertraline (Zoloft).
    c. amitriptyline (Elavil).
    d. fluoxine (Seralil).

5. According to cognitive therapists,
    a. irrational thought processes lead to abnormal behavior.
    b. imbalances in neurotransmitters cause abnormal behavior.
    c. suppression of id impulses leads to abnormal behavior.
    d. unconscious thoughts, coupled with cognitive distortions, lead to abnormal behavior.

6. Research suggests that all of the following are barriers that prevent ethnic minorities from utilizing mental health services, except
    a. cultural barriers.
    b. institutional barriers.
    c. economic barriers.
    d. all of the above.

7. Which of the following has gained widespread attention and support as a means of assisting individuals overcome fears and phobias?
   a. behavior therapy
   b. cognitive therapy
   c. psychoanalysis
   d. humanistic therapy

8. Which of the following may be produced by the regular use of benzodiazepines?
   a. tolerance
   b. kidney failure
   c. psychosis
   d. dyskinesia

9. A managed care system would most likely advocate for which of the following types of treatment for a depressed patient?
   a. psychoanalysis
   b. cognitive-behavioral therapy
   c. ECT
   d. inpatient care

10. Which of the following would a humanistic therapist accept as an appropriate outcome measure for a client?
    a. changes in GSR measures
    b. direct observation of the client's behavior
    c. indirect measures such as a family member's observation of the client
    d. client self-report regarding his or her state

11. Research indicates that psychotherapy is
    a. Effective.
    b. not effective.
    c. effective for only a selective group.

12. Evidence regarding the psychological treatment of low-income groups and people of color indicate that
    a. psychotherapy is helpful regardless of the cultural sensitivity of the therapist.
    b. psychotherapy is helpful only when treatment is offered in a culturally sensitive context.
    c. psychotherapy is helpful only when the therapist comes from the same cultural background as the client.
    d. psychotherapy is unsuccessful with low-income groups and with people of color.

13. Selective serotonin reuptake inhibitors (SSRIs) such as Prozac
    a. increase the availability of serotonin in the brain.
    b. decrease the availability of serotonin in the brain.
    c. increase the availability of serotonin while decreasing the availability to norepiniephrine.
    d. none of the above.

14. Systematic desensitization, modeling, and aversive conditioning are all forms of
_____.
    a. psychoanalysis
    b. humanistic therapy
    c. cognitive therapy
    d. behavioral therapy

15. ECT is a controversial treatment for depression because
    a. it remains unclear how or why it works.
    b. it results in memory loss.
    c. it sometimes causes psychosis.
    d. a and b.

16. The nerve that joins the _____ and the _____ is severed in a prefrontal lobotomy.
    a. thalamus; prefrontal cortex
    b. prefrontal cortex; frontal cortex
    c. limbic system; amygdala
    d. none of the above

17. An _____ orientation draws upon the theories and techniques espoused by two or more theoretical orientations in psychology.
    a. cognitive-behavioral
    b. eclectic
    c. biopsychosocial
    d. multitheoretical

18. Simon dreamed he owned a horse and a large farm. The unconscious material this dream symbolizes is known as the dream's _____.
    a. manifest content
    b. latent content
    c. transference material
    d. countertransference material

19. The token economy is a _____ approach based upon _____.
    a. cognitive; classical conditioning
    b. humanistic; operant conditioning
    c. behavioral; classical conditioning
    d. behavioral; operant conditioning

20. A central difference between traditional and newer forms of psychoanalysis is that
    a. newer approaches seek to uncover unconscious motives.
    b. newer approaches focus more on an individual's present relationships and encourage the individual to make adaptive behavior changes.
    c. newer approaches now seek to break down psychological defenses.
    d. newer approaches focus less on the ego.

21. The process by which clients are exposed to progressively more fearful stimuli while remaining deeply relaxed is known as _____ . This therapeutic technique is especially useful for the treatment of fears and phobias.
    a. token economy
    b. free association
    c. aversive conditioning
    d. systematic desensitization

22. According to Rogers, an effective therapist should possess four basic qualities. These include
    a. unconditional positive regard, empathy, congruence, and genuineness.
    b. unconditional positive regard, listening ability, genuineness, and empathy.
    c. listening skills, empathy, genuineness, and positive regard.
    d. empathy, genuineness, unconditional positive regard, and reflective abilities.

23. Rogers believed an effective therapist must be accepting of the client as a person, even if the therapist sometimes disagrees with the client's choices or behavior. This illustrates the importance of
    a. active listening skills.
    b. reflection.
    c. genuineness.
    d. unconditional positive regard.

24. Ellis' therapeutic approach, which includes actively disputing an individual's self-defeating belief system, is referred to as _____.
    a. client centered therapy
    b. rational emotive behavior therapy
    c. humanistic-existential therapy
    d. cognitive distortion therapy

25. Therapists who draw upon the techniques of different schools of therapy without necessarily adopting the theoretical orientations associated with these techniques are known as
    a. eclectics.
    b. REBT therapists.
    c. integrative eclectics.
    d. technical eclectics.

26. All of the following are problems associated with internet counseling, except
    a. on-line therapists may not be able to provide the more intensive services that clients need during periods of emotional crisis.
    b. it is unclear whether mental health professionals can legally provide on-line services to residents of states in which the therapists are not licensed.
    c. there is no system in place for ensuring that on-line therapists are qualified practitioners.
    d. all of the above are problems associated with on-line counseling.

27. Family therapists utilize a _____ approach to understand the dynamics of the family unit and problems, which may arise within it.
    a. cognitive
    b. systems
    c. behavioral
    d. client-centered
    e. none of the above

28. David used tranquilizers on a regular basis to help him sleep. Lately, he has been experiencing significant levels of anxiety and insomnia, which have been more distressing than what he experienced prior to taking these medications. It is likely that David is experiencing

   _____.
    a. withdrawal symptoms
    b. rebound anxiety
    c. major depression
    d. narcolepsy

29. Many community mental health centers administer transitional treatment facilities in the community such as _____, which provide a sheltered living environment to help clients gradually adjust to the community.
    a. deinstitutionalization
    b. halfway houses
    c. home health facilities
    d. managed care facilities

30. Indicated preventive interventions, which are directed toward individuals who display early signs of a mental disorder are referred to as _____ interventions.
    a. primary prevention
    b. secondary prevention
    c. tertiary prevention
    d. selective

SHORT ANSWER
Answers are found at the end of this chapter.
Answer the following short answer questions:

1. Discuss the four features of psychotherapy.
2. Describe several techniques utilized in behavioral therapy. What is behavioral therapy?
3. What is cognitive-behavioral therapy? What techniques are used in this form of therapy?
4. How does family therapy differ from other approaches?
5. What factors may explain low rates of utilization of mental health services by ethnic minorities?

VIDEO/CD-ROM
In order to obtain greater insight into the information presented in this chapter, refer to the video that accompanies it.

Video 4.1   Client-Centered Therapy: Dr. Carl Rogers

ANSWERS TO MATCHING

1. psychotherapy (p. 97)

2. REBT (p. 107)

3. cognitive distortions (p. 108)

4. managed care systems (p. 115)

5. psychopharmacology (p. 117)

6. nonspecific factors (p. 100)

7. manifest content (p. 101)

8. rebound anxiety (p. 118)

9. SSRIs (p. 119)

10. deinstitutionalization (p. 127)

11. systematic desensitization (p. 104)

12. eclectic orientation (p. 110)

13. family therapy (p. 112)

14. ECT (p. 121)

15. tricyclics (p. 119)

16. primary prevention (p. 124)

17. lithium (p. 120)

18. displacing (p. 102)

19. countertransference (p. 102)

20. latent content (p. 101)

21. modeling (p. 104)

22. client-centered therapy (p. 105)

23. unconditional positive regard (p. 105)

24. CBT (p. 109)

25. tolerance (p. 118)

26. antidepressants (p. 119)

27. psychoanalysis (p. 100)

28. resistance (p. 101)

29. token economy (p. 104)

30. empathy (p. 106)

31. meta-analysis (p. 113)

32. person-centered therapy (p. 105)

33. transference relationship (p. 102)

34. secondary prevention (p. 124)

35. neuroleptics (p. 118)

36. free association (p. 101)

37. object relations (p. 104)

38. genuineness (p. 106)

39. congruence (p. 106)

40. insight (p. 101)

ANSWERS TO MULTIPLE CHOICE QUESTIONS

1. a. free association (p. 101)

2. d. Psychotherapy involves a core fundamental system of interaction and techniques used by all therapeutic orientations. (p. 98)

3. d. countertransference. (p. 102)

4. d. fluoxine (Seralil). (p. 120)

5. a. irrational thought processes lead to abnormal behavior. (p. 107)

6. d. all of the above. (p. 126)

7. a. behavior therapy (p. 104)

8. a. tolerance (p. 118)

9. b. cognitive-behavioral therapy (p. 115)

10. d. client self-report regarding his or her state (p. 105)

11. a. effective. (p. 113)

12. b. psychotherapy is helpful only when treatment is offered in a culturally sensitive context (p. 117)

13. a. increase in the availability of serotonin in the brain. (p. 119)

14. d. behavioral therapy (p. 104)

15. d. a and b. (p. 121)

16. a. thalamus; prefrontal cortex (p. 121)

17. b. eclectic (p. 97)

18. b. latent content (p. 101)

19. d. behavioral; operant conditioning (p. 104)

20. b. newer approaches focus more on an individual's present relationships and encourage the individual to make adaptive behavior changes. (p. 102)

21. d. systematic desensitization (p. 104)

22. a. unconditional positive regard, empathy, congruence, and genuineness. (p. 105)

23. d. unconditional positive regard. (p. 105)

24. b. rational emotive behavior therapy (p. 107)

25. d. technical eclectics. (p. 110)

26. d. all of the above are problems associated with on-line counseling. (p. 111)

27. b. systems (p. 112)

28. b. rebound anxiety (p. 118)

29. b. halfway houses (p. 124)

30. b. secondary prevention (p. 124)

ANSWERS TO SHORT ANSWER QUESTIONS

1. There are four features that characterize psychotherapy. Psychotherapy involves systematic interactions between therapist and client. Therapists structure their interactions with clients to reflect their theoretical views. Secondly, psychotherapy draws upon psychological principles, research, and theory. Further, psychotherapy may address cognitive, behavioral, and emotional domains to assist clients in addressing difficulties and enhancing health. Finally, psychotherapy addresses not only abnormal behavior, but also engages clients in problem solving and personal growth. (p. 98)

2. Behavioral therapy is the systematic application of learning principles. Systematic desensitization is a behavioral technique based upon the principles of classical conditioning. Individuals are asked to develop a fear-stimulus hierarchy and progress through each step while employing relation methods. In this manner, individuals develop positive associations to stimuli that once caused them anxiety. Gradual exposure is another behavioral technique that involves direct exposure to increasingly fearful stimuli. This technique is sometimes combined with cognitive methods, which focus on replacing irrational thought patterns with calming, rational ones. In modeling, individuals learn more effective coping methods by observing others. After a period of observation, an individual may be guided to perform a target behavior and receive reinforcement for each attempt. The token economy is based upon operant conditioning principles, using rewards and punishments to shape behavior. In residential or institutional settings, a token economy system may be used to increase adaptive behavior by allowing individuals to earn tokens for performing appropriate behaviors. The tokens may then be exchanged for desired rewards. (pp. 104, 105)

3. Cognitive-behavioral therapy (CBT) combines therapeutic techniques, which focus upon helping individuals change overt behaviors in addition to changing underlying thought patterns. CBT draws on the assumption that thought patterns affect behavior and that changes in thinking patterns may lead to desirable behavioral changes. Interventions include behavioral techniques such as gradual exposure and systematic desensitization, in addition cognitive techniques, which address maladaptive thought patterns. (p. 109)

4. In family therapy, the family is the unit of treatment, which is the primary difference between this type of therapy and others that focus primarily on the individual. Family therapist use a systems approach to understanding the dynamics of the family and problems that may arise from it. Problem behaviors of individual family members are viewed as representing a breakdown within the system of communication and role relationships within the family. (p. 112)

5. According to a recent report by the U.S. Surgeon General, members of racial and ethnic minority groups typically have less access to mental health care and receive lower quality of care than do other Americans. Several factors that may account for this include a disproportionate number of minority members who are uninsured or underinsured, cultural mistrust of mental health services, institutional barriers such as the lack of transportation, cultural barriers that include different conceptions regarding mental health issues and treatment interventions, and language barriers. (pp. 125, 126)

ANSWERS TO CROSSWORD

Chapter Five

Stress, Psychological Factors, and Health

OBJECTIVES

1. Describe the features of adjustment disorders.
2. Explain what the general adaptation syndrome means.
3. Explain the significance of stress factors in health and illness, paying special attention to the role of the immune system.
4. Explain the role of acculturative stress in terms of the mental health of immigrant and native populations.
5. Discuss some of the psychological factors that moderate stress, including styles of coping, self-efficacy expectations, psychological hardiness, optimism, social support, and ethnic identity.
6. Explain the connection between psychological factors and physical disorders, including headaches, cardiovascular disease, asthma, cancer, and AIDS.

CHAPTER OUTLINE

Adjustment Disorders
Stress and Illness
      Stress and the Endocrine System
      Stress and the Immune System
      The General Adaptation Syndrome
      Stress and Life Changes
      Acculturative Stress: Making It in America
      Psychological Factors That Moderate Stress
Psychological Factors and Physical Disorders
      Headaches
      Cardiovascular Disease
      Asthma
      Cancer
      Acquired Immunodeficiency Syndrome (AIDS)
Summing Up

MATCHING

Answers are found at the end of this chapter. Match these terms and concepts with the definitions that follow:

stress	distress
health psychologist	endocrine system
psychoneuroimmunology	leukocytes
antigens	psychosomatic
mantra	AIDS
HIV	TABP
acculturation	General Adaptation Syndrome

alarm reaction
exhaustion stage
antibodies
fight-or-flight reaction
psychological hardiness
biofeedback training
transcendental meditation
emotion-focused coping
arteriosclerosis
steroids
catecholamines
melting pot theory
self-efficacy expectancies

resistance stage
hormones
adjustment disorder
problem-focused coping
locus of control
thermistor
cardiovascular disease
individual response specificity
atherosclerosis
immune system
stressor
bicultural theory
aura

1. _____ behavior pattern characterized by a sense of time urgency, competitiveness, and hostility. Associated with a higher risk of CHD

2. _____ an immunological disease caused by HIV

3. _____ a word or phrase that is repeated to induce relaxation

4. _____ a device for registering body temperature

5. _____ a demand made on an organism to adapt or adjust

6. _____ the system of glands that secrete hormones

7. _____ the first stage of the General Adaptation Syndrome

8. _____ a coping style that attempts to confront the stressor directly

9. _____ stress buffering traits characterized by commitment, control, and challenge

10. _____ the belief that individuals respond to the same stressor in different ways

11. _____ buildup of fatty deposits along artery walls

12. _____ a psychologist who studies the relationship between psychological factors and physical illness

13. _____ white blood cells

14. _____ the process of adapting to a new culture

15. _____ a coping style that does not seek to eliminate the stressor directly

16. _____ a perception of one's ability to affect outcomes

17. _____ a method of feeding back to the individual information about bodily responses so that the individual may exert greater control over these functions

18. _____ a state of physical or emotional pain

19. _____ substances that trigger an immune response

20. _____ a type of meditation that focuses on the repetition of a mantra to induce a meditative state

21. _____ the virus that causes AIDS

22. _____ a disorder that is characterized by impaired functioning or emotional distress as a response to an identified stressor

23. _____ the study of the relationship between psychological factors and the functioning of the endocrine, immune, and nervous systems

24. _____ substances that produce white blood cells which identify and target antigens for destruction

25. _____ the second stage of the General Adaptation Syndrome

26. _____ secretions produced by the endocrine system

27. _____ a disease involving hardening of the arteries

28. _____ a three-stage response to states of prolonged stress

29. _____ testosterone, estrogen, progesterone, and corticosteroids are examples

30. _____ dopamine, norepinephrine, and epinephrine are examples

31. _____ the third stage of the General Adaptation Syndrome

32. _____ a theory that suggests that psychosocial adjustment is fostered by identification with both traditional and host cultures

33. _____ the body's system of defense against disease

34. _____ a source of stress

35. _____ a theory which suggests that acculturation helps individuals adjust to living in the host culture

36. _____ expectations regarding our abilities to cope with challenges we face

37. _____ psychophysiological

38. _____ a cluster of warning sensations that precede a migraine

39. _____ the leading cause of death in the United States

40. _____ the inborn tendency to respond to a threat by either fighting or fleeing

CROSSWORD

Answers are found at the end of this chapter. Complete the following crossword puzzle to reinforce your understanding of this chapter's key terms and concepts:

ACROSS		DOWN	
3. a word that is repeated to induce relaxation	14. the second stage of the General Adaptation Syndrome	1. substances that produce white blood cells	13. the first stage of the General Adaptation Syndrome
5. an immunological disease caused by HIV	16. substances that trigger an immune response	2. the third stage of the General Adaptation Syndrome	15. associated with a higher risk of CHD
7. the virus that causes AIDS	18. secretions produced by the endocrine system	4. adapting to a new culture	17. a demand made on an organism to adjust or adapt
8. white blood cells	19. testosterone and estrogen are examples	6. a state of physical or emotional pain	
9. a perception of one's ability to affect outcomes	20. the source of stress	10. a system of glands	
12. a cluster of warning sensations that precede a migraine		11. a device for registering body temperature	

MULTIPLE CHOICE

The multiple choice questions listed will test your understanding of the material presented in the chapter. Read through each question and circle the letter representing the best answer. The answers are found at the end of this chapter.

1. Steve has had difficulty concentrating on his school work since his breakup with his girlfriend. Steve may be suffering from a mild type of psychological disorder called an _____.
   a. alarm reaction
   b. adjustment disorder
   c. dysthymic-depressive disorder
   d. stress disorder

2. During times of stress, the _____ branch of the autonomic nervous system stimulates the release of catecholamines that mobilize the body to deal with a threatening stressor.
   a. parasympathetic
   b. sympathetic
   c. central

3. Of interest to psychoneuroimmunologists, the _____ is the body's system of defense against disease.
   a. central nervous system
   b. immune system
   c. endocrine system
   d. parasymapathetic nervous system

4. Which of the following appear(s) to moderate the harmful effects of stress?
   a. social support
   b. stimulants
   c. benzodiazepines
   d. defense mechanisms

5. Bill tends to leave the room whenever his roommates attempt to discuss their concerns about his behavior. Psychologists would probably identify Bill's style of coping as
   a. problem-focused
   b. emotion-focused
   c. reactive
   d. manipulative

6. Mary believed that she performed well on her examination because of the amount of time she spent studying and her personal commitment to succeed in the course. Mary most certainly has an _____ regarding her achievements in school.
   a. internal locus of control
   b. external locus of control
   c. problem-focused orientation
   d. emotion-focused orientation

7. Also know as the 'adaptation stage,' the _____ stage of the General Adaptation Syndrome is characterized by an attempt to withstand prolonged stress and preserve resources.
    a. alarm
    b. coping
    c. exhaustion
    d. resistance

8. Physical disorders in which psychological factors are believed to play a contributing role have traditionally been termed _____.
    a. psychophysiological
    b. somatic
    c. reactive
    d. pathological

9. Debra has been characterized by her coworkers as ambitious, impatient, highly competitive, and sometimes hostile. Debra exhibits which of the following behavior patterns?
    a. Type B
    b. Type A
    c. Type C

10. Which of the following occurs during the alarm stage of the general adaptation syndrome?
    a. respiration rates decline
    b. muscle tension increases
    c. blood pressure drops
    d. cortisol is depleted

11. The stages of the general adaptation syndrome are (in order)
    a. denial, adjustment, acceptance.
    b. resistance, alarm, exhaustion.
    c. alarm, adjustment, exhaustion.
    d. alarm, resistance, exhaustion.

12. According to research in psychoneuroimmunology, acculturation reduces the risk of psychological problems.
    a. True
    b. False

13. Most of the research in psychoneuroimmunolgy is
    a. correlational in nature.
    b. experimental.
    c. based upon case studies.
    d. based upon naturalistic observation.

14. An individual may contract AIDS by all of the following, except
    a. donating blood.
    b. sharing needles.
    c. receiving a blood transfusion.
    d. sexual contact.

15. Which of the following is not a way of reducing TYPE A behavior?
    a. focus on the pleasure and beauty in things
    b. express appreciation to those who have offered support
    c. avoid grudges
    d. engage in competitive activities

16. According to current research, _____ may increase the life expectancies of breast cancer patients.
    a. social support
    b. anger management therapy
    c. biofeedback
    d. emotion-focused coping

17. Which of the following groups is more likely to die from coronary heart disease?
    a. White non-Hispanic
    b. Black non-Hispanic
    c. Hispanic
    d. Asian

18. Which of the following is not associated with an increased risk of coronary heart disease?
    a. a sedentary lifestyle
    b. psychological resilience
    c. Type A behavior pattern
    d. anger associated with hostility
    e. none of the above

19. In a study of first-year law school students, _____ was associated with better immune system response. This outcome is supported by studies of pregnant women and heart disease patients.
    a. commitment
    b. optimism
    c. challenge
    d. emotion-style coping

20. Which of the following is not associated with increased rates of survival for individuals who have suffered form a heart attack?
    a. attributing the heart attack to stress
    b. recognizing the importance of preventative health care
    c. expectancy that positive life changes would result from the event
    d. changes in philosophy of life

21. All of the following play a role in mediating the negative effects of stress, except
    a. optimism
    b. psychological hardiness
    c. a sense of efficacy
    d. TABP

22. One reason why persistent stress may eventually exhaust our capacity to cope is the
    a. continuous secretion of corticosteroids that can suppress the activity of the immune system.
    b. suppression of lipoproteins.
    c. continual activity of the parasympathetic branch of the autonomic nervous system can produce vulnerability.
    d. suppression of serotonin and dopamine.

23. Occupations that are characterized by _____ control and _____ demand have been correlated with greater risk of cardiovascular disease.
    a. high, high
    b. low, low
    c. high, low
    d. low, high

24. Meditation and progressive relaxation are psychological treatments that
    a. increase the effectiveness of the immune system.
    b. lower states of bodily arousal.
    c. stimulate sympathetic nervous system activity.
    d. none of the above.

25. Used to induce relaxation, a _____ is repeated to narrow consciousness.
    a. thermistor
    b. mantra
    c. tone
    d. mnemonic

26. During the alarm reaction stage of the General Adaptation Syndrome, the body is mobilized for defense. This response pattern is also termed
    a. adjustment.
    b. problem focused.
    c. emotion focused.
    d. fight or flight.

27. An individual's expectations regarding his or her ability to cope with challenges, to perform certain behaviors skillfully, and to produce positive changes in his or her life is referred to as _____ expectancies.
    a. self-efficacy
    b. self-motivating
    c. locus of control
    d. psychological hardiness

28. Business executives who resisted illness despite heavy burdens of stress displayed all of the following, except a
    a. high commitment to tasks.
    b. high competitiveness.
    c. high in challenge.
    d. high perceived control.

29. The principle of _____ holds that people may respond to a stressor in idiosyncratic ways. This may provide insight into diverse reactions to specific types of stress.
    a. biofeedback control
    b. individual response specificity
    c. individual response reaction
    d. G.A.S.

30. Which of the following groups has the highest rates of hypertension among individuals aged twenty to seventy-four?
    a. Non-Hispanic Black
    b. Cuban
    c. Non-Hispanic White
    d. Puerto Rican

SHORT ANSWER
Answers are found at the end of this chapter. Answer the following short answer questions:

1. Describe the General Adaptation Syndrome described by Hans Seyle.
2. How may stress impact one's health?
3. Discuss the process of acculturation and its impact upon mental health.
4. How may one's perception of control impact one's health.
5. How may mental health professionals play a role in the treatment of disease?

ANSWERS TO MATCHING

1. TABP (p. 148)

2. AIDS (p. 154)

3. mantra (p. 146)

4. thermistor (p. 145)

5. stress (p. 131)

6. endocrine system (p. 132)

7. alarm reaction (p. 135)

8. problem-focused coping (p. 140)

9. psychological hardiness (p. 141)

10. individual response specificity (p. 145)

11. atherosclerosis (p. 148)

12. health psychologist (p. 131)

13. leukocytes (p. 133)

14. acculturation (p. 138)

15. emotion-focused coping (p. 140)

16. locus of control (p. 142)

17. biofeedback training (p. 145)

18. distress (p. 131)

19. antigens (p. 133)

20. transcendental meditation (p. 146)

21. HIV (p. 154)

22. adjustment disorder (p. 131)

23. psychoneuroimmunology (p. 132)

24. antibodies (p. 133)

25. resistance stage (p. 135)

26. hormones (p. 132)

27. arteriosclerosis (p. 147)

28. General Adaptation Syndrome (p. 135)

29. steroids (p. 133)

30. catecholamines (p. 133)

31. exhaustion stage (p. 135)

ANSWERS TO MULTIPLE CHOICE QUESTIONS

1. b. adjustment disorder (p. 131)

2. b. sympathetic (p. 133)

3. b. immune system (p. 133)

4. a. social support (p. 134)

5. b. emotion-focused (p. 140)

6. a. internal locus of control (p. 142)

7. d. resistance (p. 135)

8. a. psychophysiological (p. 144)

9. b. Type A (p. 148)

10. b. muscle tension increases (p. 135)

11. d. alarm, resistance, exhaustion. (p. 135)

12. b. False (p. 138)

13. a. correlational in nature. (p. 134)

14. a. donating blood. (p. 154)

15. d. engage in competitive activities (p. 149)

16. a. social support (p. 153)

17. b. Black non-Hispanic (p. 149)

18. b. psychological resilience (p. 153)

19. b. optimism (p. 142)

20. a. attributing the heart attack to stress (p. 152)

21. d. TABP (p. 148)

22. a. continuous secretion of corticosteroids that can suppress the activity of the immune system. (p. 136)

23. d. low, high (p. 149)

24. b. lower states of bodily arousal. (p. 146)

25. b. mantra (p. 146)

26. d. fight or flight (p. 135)

27. a. self-efficacy (p. 141)

28. b. high competitiveness. (p. 142)

29. b. individual response specificity (p. 145)

30. a. Non-Hispanic Black (p. 150)

ANSWERS TO SHORT ANSWER QUESTIONS

1. The General Adaptation Syndrome (GAS), proposed by Hans Seyle, describes a biological response pattern to prolonged periods of stress. The syndrome consists of three stages, including the alarm reaction, the resistance stage, and the exhaustion stage. A perceived stressor triggers the alarm stage, which is characterized by autonomic nervous system (sympathetic division) responses. It is during this stage that the individual has a 'fight-or-flight' response, whereby the individual is mobilized for action. If the stressor persists, the individual enters the resistance or adaptation stage. It is also during this stage that the body attempts to preserve resources and renew spent energy. If the stressor continues, however, the individual may progress to the exhaustion stage. The exhaustion stage is characterized by lowered resistance and physical deterioration. Serious health problems may develop. (p. 135)

2. Stress may adversely affect the health of an individual. Stress affects many systems within the body, including the endocrine and immune systems. Several endocrine glands secrete stress hormones which, over the course of prolonged periods of stress, may have damaging effects throughout the body. This may also have a domino effect on the immune system, the body's system of defense against disease. Exposure to stress may suppress immunological functioning., resulting in greater vulnerability to common illnesses and more serious disease processes. The General Adaptation Syndrome provides a model for the understanding of the impact of stress on health. (pp. 132, 133)

3. Acculturation refers to the process of adapting to a new culture. Research related to acculturation and mental health is complex. Research pertaining to Hispanic Americans indicates that highly acculturated Hispanic women are more likely to be heavy drinkers. Third generation (highly acculturated) Mexican-American male adolescents are at a higher risk of delinquency. Research also indicates positive correlations between acculturation and smoking, in addition to psychological disorders such as depression, anxiety, and eating disorders. Confounding variables must be considered, however. Low acculturation status is often a marker for low socioeconomic status, which increases the risk for the development of psychological disorders. Linguistic differences, limited opportunities, and financial hardship may result in inconsistencies in research measures. (pp. 138, 139)

4. Research indicates that a number of psychological factors may buffer the effects of stress. One such factor is perception of control. Psychologically hardy individuals who have greater resistance to the deleterious effects of stress have an internal locus of control. These individuals believe in their ability to affect outcomes and feel effectual in managing their lives. Such individuals engage in more problem-solving activities and report fewer physical symptoms than those who feel powerless over their environments. (p. 142)

5. Research indicates that psychological factors play a significant role in the development of physical disorders. Mental health professionals play a key role in the management of stress and the treatment of disease. Mental health professionals may assist the individual with issues such as coping, self-efficacy, hardiness, optimism, and the development of social support. These variables serve to buffer the individual from the negative effects of stress. Furthermore, mental health professionals play a key role in helping patients cope with the emotional consequences of a disease. Feelings of hopelessness and helplessness, which tend to hamper recovery, may be addressed in order to assist patients to fight their illness. (pp. 142, 153)

ANSWERS TO CROSSWORD

ACROSS		DOWN	
3. a word that is repeated to induce relaxation	14. the second stage of the General Adaptation Syndrome	1. substances that produce white blood cells	13. the first stage of the General Adaptation Syndrome
5. an immunological disease caused by HIV	16. substances that trigger an immune response	2. the third stage of the General Adaptation Syndrome	15. associated with a higher risk of CHD
7. the virus that causes AIDS	18. secretions produced by the endocrine system	4. adapting to a new culture	17. a demand made on an organism to adjust or adapt
8. white blood cells	19. testosterone and estrogen are examples	6. a state of physical or emotional pain	
9. a perception of one's ability to affect outcomes	20. the source of stress	10. a system of glands	
12. a cluster of warning sensations that precede a migraine		11. a device for registering body temperature	

CHAPTER SIX

ANXIETY DISORDERS

OBJECTIVES

1. Define anxiety and describe the historical connection with the term neurosis.
2. Define and describe panic disorder, and explain the differences between panic attacks and other forms of anxiety.
3. Define and describe generalized anxiety disorder.
4. Define and describe specific phobia, social phobia, and agoraphobia.
5. Define and describe obsessive-compulsive disorder.
6. Describe the features of acute and posttraumatic stress disorder.
7. Describe various theoretical perspectives on the anxiety disorders.
8. Describe the various treatment approaches for anxiety disorders.
9. Discuss learning-based approaches to the treatment of anxiety disorders, including systematic desensitization, gradual exposure, flooding, cognitive therapy, virtual therapy, and cognitive-behavioral therapy.

CHAPTER OUTLINE

Types of Anxiety Disorders
    Panic Disorder
    Generalized Anxiety Disorder
    Phobic Disorders
    Obsessive-Compulsive Disorder
    Acute and Posttraumatic Stress Disorders
    Ethnic Differences in Anxiety Disorders
Theoretical Perspectives
    Psychodynamic Perspectives
    Learning Perspectives
    Cognitive Factors in Anxiety Disorders
    Biological Factors in Anxiety Disorders
    Tying It Together
Treatment of Anxiety Disorders
    Psychodynamic Approaches
    Humanistic Approaches
    Biological Approaches
    Learning-Based Approaches
Summing Up

MATCHING

Answers are found at the end of this chapter. Match these terms and concepts with the definitions that follow:

systematic desensitization	claustrophobia
breathing retraining	phobias
neuroticism	fear stimulus hierarchy
compulsion	social phobia
virtual therapy	fear
flooding	etiology
anxiety sensitivity	worry circuit
agoraphobia	obsession
gradual exposure	sodium lactate
Mowrer's two factor model	prepared conditioning
benzodiazepines	projection/displacement
gamma-aminobutyric acid	generalized anxiety disorder
acute stress disorder	cognitive restructuring
Prozac	limbic system
low self-efficacy	EMDR
exposure with response prevention	amydala
anxiety	acrophobia
hyperventilation	CBT
self-monitoring	Valium
psychodynamic perspective	panic disorder

1._____ a treatment in which the client applies counterconditioning to the imagined presence of successive stimuli in a fear-stimulus hierarchy

2._____ persistent fears disproportionate to the threat posed by stimuli that elicit them

3._____ the causes of a disorder; often forms the basis for classification

4._____ intense, irrational fear of being out in open, busy areas

5._____ a class of minor tranquilizers commonly used to reduce anxiety and tension

6._____ irresistible, repetitive urge to perform a specific action

7._____ psychodynamic defense mechanisms theoretically involved in the development of phobias

8._____ the extent to which a person believes that his or her emotional or physical arousal will lead to harmful consequences

9._____ the process therapists use to help clients pinpoint their self-defeating thoughts and generate rational alternatives

10._____ a neural network in the brain that signals danger

11._____ induces feelings of panic in some people, especially in people with panic disorder

12._____ intense, irrational fear of being negatively judged by others

13._____ stimuli that are ordered in a sequence, according to their ability to evoke anxiety

14._____ a treatment approach that has the client maintain a state of calmness while being
exposed to the phobic stimuli

15._____ a genetically linked trait that may be an etiological factor in the development of
anxiety

16._____ stress reaction occurring shortly after a traumatic event

17._____ an "inhibitory" neurotransmitter that regulates nervous activity

18._____ a cognitive-behavioral treatment for panic disorder that
aims at restoring a normal level of carbon dioxide in the client's blood

19._____ the fear of a neutral object learned through classical conditioning and maintained
through operant avoidance

20._____ the feeling of anxiety and agitation in response to a threat

21._____ a type of exposure therapy in which the client is exposed to intensely anxiety-
provoking situations

22._____ characterized by persistent feelings of anxiety that are not associated with a specific
object, situation, or activity

23._____ recurring, uncontrollable thoughts that create anxiety sufficient to interfere with
daily life

24._____ the fear of enclosed spaces

25._____ a new treatment approach, using a computer-generated simulated environment as a
method of gradual exposure

26._____ the idea that people may be genetically prepared to acquire phobic responses to
certain classes of stimuli

27._____ used in the treatment of obsessive-compulsive disorder; also known as fluoxetine

28. _____ a system within the brain that plays a key role in memory formation and the processing of emotional responses

29. _____ lack of belief in one's ability to perform tasks successfully

30. _____ a new and controversial treatment for PTSD

31. _____ used in the treatment of OCD; individuals with OCD learn to tolerate the anxiety triggered by their obsession while they are prevented from performing their compulsive rituals

32. _____ located in the limbic system, it is involved in processing threatening stimuli

33. _____ an emotional state characterized by physiological arousal

34. _____ fear of heights

35. _____ a pattern of overly rapid breathing

36. _____ a type of therapy which incorporates behavioral and cognitive techniques

37. _____ keeping a log of behavioral responses to help determine stimuli that may trigger them

38. _____ also known as diazepam, this medication is used to treat anxiety disorders

39. _____ from this perspective, anxiety is a danger signal that threatening impulses of a sexual or aggressive nature are nearing awareness

40. _____ involves the occurrence of repeated, unexpected panic attacks

CROSSWORD

Answers are found at the end of this chapter. Complete the following crossword puzzle to reinforce your understanding of this chapter's key terms and concepts:

ACROSS	DOWN
1. limbic structure that processes threatening stimuli	1. fear of heights
2. fluoxetine	2. persistent fear disproportionate to threat
4. irrational fear of open spaces	3. incorporates behavioral and cognitive techniques
6. overly rapid breathing	5. involves recurrent panic attacks
10. neural network that signals danger	7. new and controversial treatment of PTSD
11. recurring thought	8. causes of a disorder
14. feelings of anxiety in response to threat	9. a repetitive action
15. type of exposure therapy	12. emotional state characterized by physiological arousal
	13. diazepam
	16. an inhibitory neurotransmitter

MULTIPLE CHOICE

Answers are found at the end of this chapter. The multiple choice questions listed will test your understanding of the material presented in the chapter. Read through each question and circle the letter representing the best answer.

1. Which of the following statements is true regarding specific phobias?
    a. Specific phobias are characterized by general anxiety symptoms.
    b. Men are more likely to develop specific phobias.
    c. Specific phobias are among the most common psychological disorders.
    d. Specific phobias are extremely rare.

2. According to which theory is anxiety caused by the social repression of our genuine selves?
    a. psychodynamic
    b. cognitive
    c. behavioral
    d. humanistic

3. All of the following are physical features of anxiety, except
    a. excessive verbalization.
    b. sweaty palms.
    c. heavy perspiration.
    d. dizziness.

4. Which of the following is the most logical first step in helping a client to develop a fear-stimulus hierarchy to alleviate the fear of riding in elevators?
    a. standing outside the elevator
    b. standing in the elevator with the door closed
    c. taking the elevator up one floor
    d. taking the elevator down to the basement

5. Which of the following is the new and controversial technique used in the treatment of PTSD that may be nothing more than just a novel way of conducting exposure-based therapy?
    a. relaxation training
    b. biofeedback
    c. visual image processing (VIP)
    d. eye movement desensitization and reprocessing (EMDR)

6. If parents squirm, grimace, or shudder at a spider crawling on the floor, their children
    a. may learn to respond to spiders with fear and avoidance behavior.
    b. will eventually develop panic attacks in response to spiders.
    c. will most likely ignore the parents' reaction and only develop fears in reaction to their own experiences.
    d. none of the above.

7. Most compulsions fall into which two categories?
   a. morning rituals and bedtime rituals
   b. checking rituals and counting rituals
   c. mealtime rituals and cleaning rituals
   d. checking rituals and cleaning rituals

8. Which of the following wartime stressors was associated with the greatest likelihood of developing PTSD symptomatology for both men and women?
   a. exposure to traditional combat
   b. the sense of threat
   c. exposure to atrocities or extreme violence
   d. the experience of living in a harsh, stressful, and unpleasant environment

9. Which of the following are not true of panic disorder?
   a. A panic disorder is associated with a strong sense of uncontrollability.
   b. First attacks typically occur spontaneously or unexpectedly.
   c. There are significant physical differences between cued and uncued panic attacks, and it is therefore easy to distinguish them.
   d. Panic disorder is often associated with agoraphobia.

10. Which of the following is not a subtype of specific phobias?
    a. blood-injection-injury type
    b. survivor guilt type
    c. animal type
    d. natural environment type

11. Which of the following is not an element of cognitive-behavioral treatment of panic disorder?
    a. self-monitoring
    b. exposure
    c. insight
    d. development of coping responses

12. Which of the following treatment focuses on altering a client's self-defeating thoughts and beliefs?
    a. cognitive approaches
    b. psychodynamic approaches
    c. behavioral approaches
    d. existential-humanistic approaches

13. Which of the following psychologists developed systematic desensitization on the assumption that maladaptive anxiety responses are learned or conditioned?
    a. Albert Ellis
    b. Joseph Wolpe
    c. Albert Bandura
    d. O. Hobart Mowrer

14. Anxiety disorders were classified as neuroses in the first two editions of the DSM. This was largely due to
    a. the assumption that anxiety disorders had underlying biological causes.
    b. anxiety disorders being grouped with more serious disturbances.
    c. Freud's view that anxiety disorders represented various ways of protecting the ego from anxiety.
    d. anxiety disorders being highly resilient to treatment.

15. Which of the following factors most likely lessened the incidence of PTSD in Vietnam veterans?
    a. if the veteran was married
    b. if the veteran was divorced
    c. if the veteran had lower intelligence
    d. if the veteran had already experienced trauma prior to combat

16. In treating anxiety disorders, humanistic approaches
    a. aim at helping people get in touch with and express their genuine talents and feelings.
    b. help the client explore sources of anxiety that arise from current relationships.
    c. would utilize systematic desensitization in working with the client.
    d. help the client to identify and resolve unconscious conflict.

17. According to the psychodynamic perspective, panic disorder is a result of
    a. an overprediction of fear, which leads to avoidance.
    b. desperate attempts of the ego to repress sexual or aggressive impulses that approach the boundaries of consciousness.
    c. a vicious cycle resulting from misinterpretation of bodily sensations.
    d. the fear that repressed impulses might become conscious.

18. In a study conducted by the Epidemiologic Catchment Area (ECA), it was found that both African-Americans and Hispanic-Americans were more likely than their non-Hispanic white counterparts to develop _____ but were less likely to develop _____.
    a. generalized anxiety disorder, PTSD
    b. phobic disorders, panic disorder
    c. obsessive compulsive disorders, social phobias
    d. PTSD, phobic disorders

19. All of the following are true of using drug therapy to treat panic disorder, except
    a. the client may attribute improvement to the drug and not to their own resources.
    b. relapses are common following discontinuation of the drug.
    c. it is more effective if cognitive techniques are incorporated with the drug therapy.
    d. there have been no problems identified in using drug therapy to treat panic disorder.

20. Which of the following anxiety disorders affect men and women in about equal numbers?
    a. social phobia
    b. agoraphobia
    c. obsessive-compulsive disorder
    d. panic disorder

21. A person who feels capable of performing a task such as giving a speech in public is an example of someone with
    a. anxiety insensitivity.
    b. a high self-efficacy expectancy.
    c. an irrational belief.
    d. a displace aggressive impulse.

22. Cognitive therapists attribute obsessive-compulsive disorder to
    a. an irrational concern about broad life themes, such as finances, health, and family matters.
    b. tendencies to exaggerate the risk of negative outcomes and to adopt irrational beliefs.
    c. hidden, unconscious conflicts.
    d. a manifestation of unmet needs.

23. Behavior therapy has been successful in treating obsessive-compulsive disorder with carefully monitored programs that include a combination of
    a. exposure with response prevention.
    b. systematic desensitization with worry reduction training.
    c. flooding with breathing retraining.
    d. cognitive restructuring with thought prevention training.

24. All of the following are cognitive features of anxiety, except
    a. fear of losing control.
    b. preoccupation with bodily sensations.
    c. clinging, dependent behavior.
    d. worrying about every little thing.

25. Which of the following neurotransmitters regulates nervous activity by preventing neurons from overly exciting their neighbors:
    a. serotonin
    b. norepinephrine
    c. GABA
    d. dopamine

26. In exposure therapy, people with social phobias are instructed to
    a. enter increasingly stressful social situations and remain in those situations until their urge to escape has lessened.
    b. visualize themselves in a stressful social situation and practice relaxation breathing until their anxiety decreases.
    c. enter increasingly stressful social situations and remain in those situations until their urge to escape has become too great to stay any longer.
    d. identify the stressful components that comprise their anxiety in social situations and work on decreasing the stress associated with these components, one at a time.

27. Which drug(s) has obsessive-compulsive disorder been shown to respond best to?
    a. tranquilizers
    b. MAO inhibitors
    c. SSRI-type antidepressants
    d. phenothiazines

28. Which of the following statements is true about anxiety disorders?
    a. People frequently meet diagnostic criteria for more than one anxiety disorder.
    b. William Cullen was the first to propose that anxiety disorders had primarily psychological origins.
    c. Anxiety disorders are mutually exclusive.
    d. People who are psychotic rarely experience anxiety.

29. Cognitive models of panic disorder assume that panic attacks arise from
    a. low self-esteem.
    b. an unusually sensitive suffocation alarm system.
    c. catastrophic misinterpretations of bodily sensations, such as dizziness and heart palpitations.
    d. overprediction of fearful situations.

30. Freud's historic case of "Little Hans," a little boy afraid of being bitten by a horse, was an illustration of Freud's principle of
    a. repression.
    b. rationalization.
    c. dissociation.
    d. displacement.

SHORT ANSWER

Answers are found at the end of this chapter. Answer the following short answer questions:

1. What physical, psychological, and behavioral features are associated with anxiety?
2. Discuss ethnic differences in anxiety disorders.
3. List and describe the five major types of anxiety disorders.
4. Discuss several behavioral factors that may give rise to anxiety disorders.
5. What interventions are available for the treatment of anxiety disorders?

VIDEO/CD-ROM

In order to gain greater insight into the information presented in this chapter, refer to the videos that accompany it.

Video 6.1   Panic Disorder: The Case of Jerry
Video 6.2   Obsessive-Compulsive Disorder: The Case of Ed

ANSWERS TO MATCHING

1. systematic desensitization (p. 184)

2. phobias (p. 164)

3. etiology (p. 161)

4. agoraphobia (p. 167)

5. benzodiazepines (p. 180)

6. compulsion (p.169)

7. projection/displacement (p. 174)

8. anxiety sensitivity (p. 177)

9. cognitive restructuring (p. 187)

10. worry circuit (p. 181)

11. sodium lactate (p. 180)

12. social phobia (p. 166)

13. fear stimulus hierarchy (p. 184)

14. gradual exposure (p. 185)

15. neuroticism (p. 180)

16. acute stress disorder (p. 170)

17. gamma-aminobutyric acid (p. 180)

18. breathing retraining (p. 190)

19. Mowrer's two factor model (p. 174)

20. fear (p. 184)

21. flooding (p. 186)

22. generalized anxiety disorder (p. 163)

23. obsession (p. 168)

24. claustrophobia (p. 165)

25. virtual therapy (p. 188)

26. prepared conditioning (p. 175)

27. Prozac (p. 184)

28. limbic system (p. 181)

29. low self-efficacy (p. 178)

30. EMDR (p. 190)

31. exposure with response prevention (p. 189)

32. amygdala (p. 181)

33. anxiety (p. 159)

34. acrophobia (p. 165)

35. hyperventilation (p. 180)

36. CBT (p. 188)

37. self-monitoring (p. 191)

38. Valium (p. 183)

39. psychodynamic perspective (p. 174)

40. panic disorder (p. 162)

ANSWERS TO MULTIPLE CHOICE QUESTIONS

1. c. Specific phobias are among the most common psychological disorders. (p. 166)

2. d. humanistic (p. 183)

3. a. excessive verbalization. (p. 160)

4. a. standing outside the elevator (p. 184)

5. d. eye movement desensitization and reprocessing (p. 190)

6. a. may learn to respond to spiders with fear and avoidance behavior. (p. 175)

7. d. checking rituals and cleaning rituals (p. 169)

8. d. the experience of living in a harsh, stressful, and unpleasant environment (p. 170)

9. c. There are significant physical differences between cued and uncued panic attacks, and it is therefore easy to distinguish them. (p. 162)

10. b. survivor guilt type (p. 165)

11. c. insight (p. 188)

12. a. cognitive approaches (p. 188)

13. b. Joseph Wolpe (p. 184)

14. c. Freud's view that anxiety disorders represented various ways of protecting the ego from anxiety. (p. 161)

15. a. if the veteran was married (p. 170)

16. a. aim at helping people get in touch with, and express, their genuine talents and feelings. (p. 183)

17. d. the fear that repressed impulses might become conscious. (p. 174)

18. b. phobic disorders, panic disorder (p. 173)

19. d. there have been no problems identified in using drug therapy to treat panic disorder. (p. 183)

20. c. obsessive-compulsive disorder (p. 169)

21. b. a high self-efficacy expectancy. (p. 178)

22. b. tendencies to exaggerate the risk of negative outcomes and to adopt irrational beliefs. (p. 177)

23. a. exposure with response prevention. (p. 189)

24. c. clinging, dependent behavior. (p. 160)

25. c. GABA (p. 180)

26. a. enter increasingly stressful social situations and remain in those situations until the urge to escape has lessened. (p. 189)

27. c. SSRI-type antidepressants (p. 184)

28. a. People meet diagnostic criteria for more than one anxiety disorder. (p. 161)

29. c. catastrophic misinterpretations of bodily sensations, such as dizziness and heart palpitations. (p. 178)

30. d. displacement. (p. 174)

ANSWERS TO SHORT ANSWER QUESTIONS

1. Anxiety disorders are characterized by myriad of physical, cognitive, and behavioral features. The physical features related to anxiety are often the result of autonomic activity discussed in previous chapters. An individual with anxiety may experience heavy perspiration, shortness of breath, light headedness, upset stomach, heart palpitations, and feelings of irritability. Behavioral features of anxiety may include dependent or agitated behavior. The individual may also engage in avoidance behavior in an attempt to reduce symptomatology. The presence of worry and fear are significant cognitive features of anxiety. The individual may experience a sense of dread or apprehension regarding the future, fear losing control, or experience repetitive thoughts. As such, an individual with anxiety may have difficulties concentrating and coping. (p.160)

2. Anxiety disorders are not unique to Western culture. Multinational research has indicated rates of panic disorder as relatively consistent across several countries. Although rates of anxiety disorders may be similar across cultures, specific features may vary. Within the United States, rates of anxiety disorders are generally similar across racial and ethnic groupings. Trivial differences may be found dependent upon age. (p. 173)

3. Anxiety disorders include panic disorder, generalized anxiety disorder, phobic disorders, obsessive-compulsive disorders, and traumatic stress disorders. Panic disorder is characterized by the occurrence of repeated, unexpected panic attacks. Panic attacks are episodes of terror experienced by an individual, accompanied by significant physiological symptoms, thoughts of danger, feelings of dread, and urge to escape. Generalized anxiety disorder involves general or persistent anxiety across situations. As such, an individual may experience heightened states of physiological arousal with accompanying behavioral and cognitive symptoms throughout the day. This is in contrast to phobic disorders, whereby anxiety is experienced in response to a specific situation or object. Obsessive-compulsive disorder is characterized by recurrent thoughts (obsessions) and/or repetitive behaviors (compulsions). Obsessive thoughts typically generate anxiety for the individual who is often partially relieved through compulsive behavior. Traumatic disorders include acute stress disorder and posttraumatic stress disorder. Acute stress disorder involves an acute maladaptive reaction in the immediate aftermath of a trauma, whereas posttraumatic stress disorder is characterized by a prolonged maladaptive reaction to a traumatic event. (pp. 162-172)

4. Behavioral psychologists believe anxiety disorders are the result of conditioning or learning. Anxiety disorders are viewed within the context of operant and classical conditioning principles. Mowrer's two factor model is useful in this regard. The fear component of an anxiety disorder may be understood as the result of classical conditioning. An individual may learn to associate a previously neutral stimulus with a stimulus that triggers a fear response. Once fear is established, the avoidance response is maintained by operant conditioning principles. Through avoidance, the individual removes an unpleasant or fear inducing stimulus. By doing so, the individual is negatively reinforced and therefore apt to repeat the same avoidance response. (pp. 174, 175)

5. Several interventions for the treatment of anxiety disorders are available. Included are psychopharmacological interventions, which serve to control the anxiety symptoms themselves; cognitive-behavioral approaches, which focus on cognitive restructuring to change maladaptive thought patterns; psychodynamic interventions, which address underlying conflicts that may give rise to symptoms of anxiety; behavioral interventions which address associations made between stimuli and reward contingencies; and humanistic approaches, which assist the individual in accepting genuine feelings and needs. (pp. 183-192)

ANSWERS TO CROSSWORD

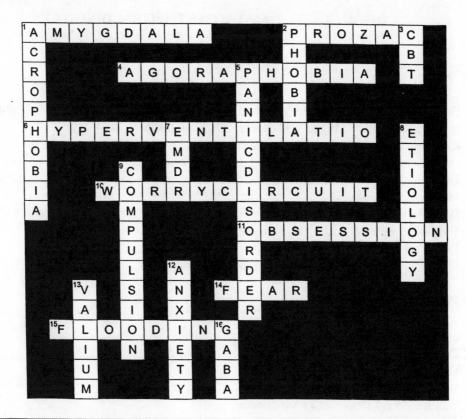

	ACROSS
1.	limbic structure that processes threatening stimuli
2.	fluoxetine
4.	irrational fear of open spaces
6.	overly rapid breathing
10.	neural network that signals danger
11.	recurring thought
14.	feelings of anxiety in response to threat
15.	type of exposure therapy

	DOWN
1.	fear of heights
2.	persistent fear disproportionate to threat
3.	incorporates behavioral and cognitive techniques
5.	involves recurrent panic attacks
7.	new and controversial treatment of PTSD
8.	causes of a disorder
9.	a repetitive action
12.	emotional state characterized by physiological arousal
13.	diazepam
16.	an inhibitory neurotransmitter

CHAPTER SEVEN

DISSOCIATIVE AND SOMATOFORM DISORDERS

OBJECTIVES

1. Describe the major features of dissociative disorders, including dissociative identity, dissociative amnesia, dissociative fugue, and depersonalization disorder.
2. Recount various theoretical perspectives on the dissociative disorders.
3. Describe various methods for treating dissociative disorders.
4. Differentiate between malingering and factitious disorder, and describe the symptoms of Munchausen syndrome.
5. Describe the features of somatoform disorders, including conversion disorder, hypochondriasis, body dysmorphic disorder, and somatization disorder.
6. Discuss theoretical perspectives of somatoform disorders.
7. Distinguish somatoform disorders from malingering.

CHAPTER OUTLINE

Dissociative Disorders
      Dissociative Identity Disorder
      Dissociative Amnesia
      Dissociative Fugue
      Culture-Bound Dissociative Syndromes
      Theoretical Perspectives
      Tying it Together
      Treatment of Dissociative Disorders
Somatoform Disorders
      Conversion Disorder
      Hypochondriasis
      Body Dysmorphic Disorder
      Somatization Disorder
      Focus on Diversity: Koro and Dhat Syndromes: Far Eastern Somatoform Disorders?
      Theoretical Perspectives
      Treatment of Somatoform Disorders
Summing Up

MATCHING

Answers are found at the end of this chapter. Match these terms and concepts with the definitions that follow:

somatoform disorders
recovered memories
hypochondriasis
selective amnesia
self-handicapping strategy
dissociative fugue
primary gains
derealization
conversion disorder
Munchausen syndrome
somatization disorder
localized amnesia
SSRIs
body dysmorphic disorder
zar
OCD
dissociative identity disorder
social reinforcement model
fugue
PTSD

dissociative amnesia
la belle indifference
dissociative disorders
Dhat syndrome
depersonalization disorder
DES
factitious disorder
psychogenic amnesia
malingering
Koro syndrome
diathesis-stress model
generalized amnesia
secondary gains
amok
Briquet's syndrome
hysteria
alternate personalities
split personality
childhood sexual abuse
memory

1. _____ disorders showing physical symptoms without organic basis or anxiety

2. _____ amnesia for specific details of a stressful event

3. _____ proposes that certain personality traits may predispose individuals to develop dissociative experiences when under extreme stress

4. _____ a controversial issue; psychologist Elizabeth Loftus is a leading researcher in this area

5. _____ recurrent and multiple physical complaints that usually involve different organ systems in the absence of organic abnormalities

6. _____ disorders showing psychological difficulties without manifest anxiety

7. _____ the fear that genitals are shrinking and retracting into one's body

8. _____ an apparent lack of concern about a conversion disorder symptom

9. _____ used to measure dissociative experiences in general population and in those with dissociative disorders

10. _____ an abnormal fear that a physical symptom is due to an underlying
serious illness

11. _____ dissociative amnesia with a change of location and a new identity

12. _____ loss of a sensory or motor function without physical cause

13. _____ a sudden loss of memory not attributable to physical problems

14. _____ dissociative amnesia for a fixed period of time following a trauma

15. _____ according to psychodynamic theory, this typically allows an individual to keep
internal conflicts repressed

16. _____ an inability to remember any of the details of one's life

17. _____ now known as dissociative amnesia

18. _____ may be helpful in treating depersonalization disorder

19. _____ consciously and deliberately faking symptoms to obtain rewards

20. _____ excessive fears over the loss of seminal fluid during nocturnal
emission, often associated with sexual difficulties

21. _____ marked changes in the perception of one's surroundings or time

22. _____ intentional fabrication of symptoms with no apparent goal

23. _____ typically allows individuals to avoid burdensome or difficult responsibilities and
gain the support from others around them

24. _____ a specific type of factitious disorder when persons tell outrageous
lies to physicians and subject themselves to unnecessary medical
procedures

25. _____ recurrent feelings of detachment from one's body

26. _____ cognitive theorists speculate that hypochondriasis my represent this

27. _____ preoccupation with an imagined or exaggerated physical defect

28. _____ a trancelike state in which a person suddenly becomes highly excited and violently
attacks others or destroys objects

29. _____ spirit possession in people who experience dissociative states

30. _____ now known as somatization disorder

31. _____ a dissociative disorder in which a person has two or more distinct personalities

32. _____ learning theorists link this disorder with hypochondriasis and body dysmorphic disorder

33. _____ also known as alter personalities, these may show different EEG records, allergic reactions, and responses to medication

34. _____ a model that helps to explain why some clinicians seem to 'discover' many more cases of multiple personality than others

35. _____ refers to multiple personality and not to schizophrenia

36. _____ derives from the Latin 'fugere,' meaning flight

37. _____ plays a pivotal role in the etiology of multiple personality

38. _____ people who are low in fantasy proneness may experience the kind of anxious, intrusive thought pattern characteristic of this disorder, rather than dissociative experiences

39. _____ a reconstructive process

40. _____ now referred to as conversion disorder

CROSSWORD

Answers are found at the end of this chapter. Complete the following crossword puzzle to reinforce your understanding of this chapter's key terms and concepts:

ACROSS	DOWN

ACROSS

3. a reconstructive process
6. 'flight'
7. plays pivotal role in etiology of multiple personality
8. spirit possession in those who experience dissociative states
12. abnormal fear that physical symptom is result of serious underlying illness
14. linked with BDD
15. fear that genitals are shrinking

DOWN

1. disorders involving physical symptoms without an organic basis
2. amnesia for specific details of an event
4. deliberately faking symptoms
5. changes in the perceptions of one's surroundings or time
6. disorder involving fabrication of symptoms with no apparent goal
9. now referred to as conversion disorder
10. fears over loss of seminal fluid
11. now known as somatization disorder
13. preoccupation with an imagined physical defect

MULTIPLE CHOICE

Answers are found at the end of this chapter. The multiple choice questions listed will test your understanding of the material presented in the chapter. Read through each question and circle the letter representing the best answer.

1. The first two DSM's grouped anxiety, dissociative, and somatoform disorders together because
    a. the learning perspective assumes that all of these disorders are due to anxiety.
    b. the psychodynamic perspective assumes that all of these disorders are due to anxiety.
    c. the cognitive perspective assumes that all of these disorders result from a lack of meaning in one's life.
    d. the psychodynamic perspective assumes that all of these disorders result from either heterophobia or homophobia.

2. Research on dissociative identity disorder suggests that
    a. the frequency of this disorder is stable across Western countries.
    b. the disorder has become less frequent in our culture in the last twenty years.
    c. the disorder appears to be culture bound and restricted to North America.
    d. the disorder is more prevalent in Japan than North America.

3. This disorder was formerly identified as "Multiple Personality Disorder" in previous editions of the DSM:
    a. dissociative fugue
    b. dissociative identity disorder
    c. dissociative amnesia
    d. depersonalization disorder

4. Diagnosis of a conversion disorder
    a. requires the presence of multiple physical symptoms.
    b. always involves a loss of sexual functioning.
    c. is a relatively straightforward diagnosis to make and is not hard to differentiate from medical disorders.
    d. should be considered in the case of a false pregnancy.

5. Epidemiological research on somatization disorder suggests that
    a. it is more frequently diagnosed in women.
    b. it usually begins in adolescence or early adulthood.
    c. it is a lifelong disorder.
    d. all of the above.

6. Which of the following models helps explain why some clinicians seem to "discover" more cases of Multiple Personality Disorder than others?
    a. cognitive-behavioral model
    b. social observation model
    c. social reinforcement model
    d. none of the above

7. A symptom that may be present in both dissociative identity disorder and schizophrenia is
    a. split affect.
    b. auditory hallucinations.
    c. thought disorder.
    d. localized amnesia.

8. The DSM suggests that the majority of young adults will encounter the feeling that they are detached from their bodies or minds. They are not diagnosed as having a depersonalization disorder because
    a. they are too young to be diagnosed.
    b. depersonalization only involves emotions.
    c. the detachment is only temporary.
    d. young adults are never disturbed by the experience.

9. Persons suffering from conversion disorder differ from persons malingering in that, persons suffering from a conversion disorder
    a. are not consciously inventing symptoms.
    b. are more likely to be blind.
    c. have symptoms with a definite organic basis.
    d. receive no secondary gains.

10. Many clinicians are reluctant to make a diagnosis of dissociative identity disorder because
    a. its features overlap with other disorders.
    b. it is considered rare.
    c. there are few clinicians who have been trained and are qualified to make the diagnosis.
    d. a and b.
    e. b and c

11. The individual personalities of a person suffering from a dissociative identity disorder are
    a. usually schizophrenic.
    b. present at the same time.
    c. well integrated.
    d. always aware of each other.

12. Memory should be thought of as
   a. a reconstructive process in which bits of information are pieced together in a way that is sometimes distorted.
   b. a mental camera that stores accurate snapshots of events.
   c. an unreliable process that should never be trusted.
   d. accurate when objective information is being processed, but less reliable when emotional information is being stored.

13. Which feature would not be considered a risk factor for the possible presence of dissociative identity disorder?
   a. severe physical or sexual abuse in childhood
   b. a parent with a diagnosis of schizophrenia
   c. suggestibility to hypnotic suggestions
   d. a stormy history of psychological treatment

14. Persons with somatization disorder are more anxious about _____ than are hypochondriacs.
   a. symptoms
   b. problems in interpersonal relationships
   c. failure
   d. memory loss

15. A limitation of the psychodynamic theory of hysteria is that
   a. the theory does not clearly distinguish primary from secondary gain.
   b. the theory does not explain how hysterical symptoms are functional.
   c. the theory does not explain how energies left over from unconscious conflicts become transformed into physical complaints.
   d. all of the above.

16. Which of the following is not a symptom of a dissociative fugue?
   a. loss of memory for the past
   b. assumption of a new identity
   c. sudden travel from home
   d. a schizophrenic new personality

17. A difference between a malingerer and a person with Munchausen disorder is that
   a. the malingerer will engage in more dramatic behavior to convince others that he or she is truly ill.
   b. the person with Munchausen disorder may be unaware of the underlying motives for his or her behavior.
   c. the malingerer is more likely to have a childhood history of hospitalizations.
   d. the person with Munchausen disorder is more likely to "give up" when confronted with evidence of his or her deception.

18. According to psychodynamic theory, the process of dissociation is
    a. an ego-driven processing of fantasy material.
    b. a coping mechanism that serves to integrate fantasy and reality.
    c. a psychological defense involving a splitting-off of consciousness to
       block out unacceptable memories or impulses.
    d. warding off psychological anxiety through the manifestation of
       physical symptoms.

19. If a person is unable to remember anything about the week after his or her father died, he or she has what type of dissociative amnesia?
    a. continuous amnesia
    b. generalized amnesia
    c. localized amnesia
    d. selective amnesia

20. Depersonalization disorder differs from the other dissociative disorders in that depersonalization
    a. involves no memory disturbance.
    b. produces little distress for the person.
    c. symptoms are long lasting.
    d. occurs more frequently in females.

21. A dissociative fugue state usually ends
    a. quite suddenly.
    b. after shock therapy.
    c. after several weeks of taking medication.
    d. gradually, over the course of several years.

22. Research suggests that exposure to _____ is involved in the development of dissociative disorders.
    a. other people with dissociative disorders
    b. parental divorce prior to the age of 3
    c. trauma
    d. none of the above

23. The behavioral approach to treating somatoform disorders may include
    a. teaching family members to reward attempts to assume responsibility
       and ignore complaining.
    b. focusing on removing sources of secondary reinforcement that may
       become connected with physical complaints.
    c. helping the person learn more effective ways of coping with anxiety.
    d. all of the above.

24. All of the following personality traits may predispose an individual to develop dissociative experiences when faced with extremely stressful situations, except
    a. high hypnotizability.
    b. fantasy proneness.
    c. shy and introverted.
    d. openness to altered states of consciousness.

25. An example of a fleeting dissociative experience would be
    a. feeling dizzy or faint.
    b. experiencing chest pains.
    c. the feeling that your leg has fallen asleep.
    d. finding yourself in a place and not knowing how you got there.

26. Munchausen Syndrome is a form of
    a. factitious disorder.
    b. conversion disorder.
    c. hypochondriasis.
    d. somatization disorder.

27. All of the following are true of hypochondriasis except
    a. the individual consciously fakes his or her symptoms.
    b. no organic basis of the symptoms can be found.
    c. fear of serious illness persists despite medical reassurance that the fears are unjustified.
    d. it is equally common in men and women.
    e. all of the above are true

28. Psychodynamic and learning theories concur that the symptoms in conversion disorder
    a. are due to childhood trauma.
    b. are not functional.
    c. are due to observational learning.
    d. relieve anxiety.

29. Cognitive therapists have speculated that some cases of hypochondriasis may represent a type of
    a. self-handicapping strategy.
    b. mood disorder.
    c. antisocial personality type.
    d. diathesis.

30. Psychodynamic and learning therapists agree that the symptoms in conversion disorders
    a. represent a diathesis.
    b. relieve anxiety.
    c. represent internalized conflict.
    d. none of the above.

SHORT ANSWER

Answers are found at the end of this chapter. Answer the following short answer questions:

1. Discuss the major types of dissociative disorders and their clinical features.
2. Discuss the major types of somatoform disorders and their clinical features.
3. What role does anxiety play in the development of dissociative and somatoform disorders?
4. Discuss the controversy regarding the diagnosis of dissociative identity disorder.
5. What role does child sexual abuse have in the development of dissociative disorders?

VIDEO/CD-ROM

In order to obtain greater insight into the information presented in this chapter, refer to the videos that accompany it.

Video 7.1   Dissociative Identity Disorder: The Three Faces of Eve
Video 7.2   Dissociative Identity Disorder: Dr. Holliday Milby

ANSWERS TO MATCHING

1. somatoform disorders (pp. 195, 211)

2. selective amnesia (p. 200)

3. diathesis-stress model (p. 207)

4. recovered memories (pp. 208-209)

5. somatization disorder (p. 215)

6. dissociative disorders (p. 195)

7. Koro syndrome (pp. 215-216)

8. la belle indifference (p. 212)

9. DES (p. 205)

10. hypochondriasis (p. 212)

11. dissociative fugue (p. 201)

12. conversion disorder (pp. 211-212)

13. dissociative amnesia (p. 200)

14. localized amnesia (p. 200)

15. primary gains (p. 217)

16. generalized amnesia (p. 200)

17. psychogenic amnesia (p. 200)

18. SSRIs (p. 210)

19. malingering (p. 201)

20. Dhat syndrome (p. 216)

21. derealization (p. 203)

22. factitious disorder (p. 211)

23. secondary gains (p. 217)

24. Munchausen syndrome (p. 211)

25. depersonalization disorder (pp. 203-204)

26. self-handicapping strategy (p. 218)

27. body dysmorphic disorder (p. 214)

28. amok (p. 204)

29. zar (p. 204)

30. Briquet's syndrome (p. 215)

31. dissociative identity disorder (p. 196)

32. OCD (p. 218)

33. alternate personalities (p. 196)

34. social reinforcement model (p. 199)

35. split personality (p. 200)

36. fugue (p. 201)

37. childhood sexual abuse (p. 206)

38. PTSD (p. 207)

39. memory (p. 209)

40. hysteria (p. 212)

ANSWERS TO MULTIPLE CHOICE QUESTIONS

1. b. the psychodynamic perspective assumes that all of these disorders are due to anxiety. (p. 195)

2. c. the disorder appears to be culture bound and restricted to North America. (p. 199)

3. b. dissociative identity disorder. (p. 196)

4. d. should be considered in the case of a false pregnancy. (p. 212)

5. d. all of the above. (p. 215)

6. c. social reinforcement model (p. 199)

7. b. auditory hallucinations. (p. 200)

8. c. the detachment is only temporary (p. 203)

9. a. are not consciously inventing symptoms. (pp. 201, 211)

10. d. a and b. (p. 199)

11. c. well integrated. (pp. 196-198)

12. a. a reconstructive process in which bits of information are pieced together in a way that is sometimes distorted. (pp. 208, 209)

13. b. a parent with a diagnosis of schizophrenia (pp. 205-207)

14. a. symptoms (p. 215)

15. c. the theory does not explain how energies left over from unconscious conflicts become transformed into physical complaints. (p. 217)

16. d. a schizophrenic new personality (p. 201)

17. b. the person with Munchausen disorder may be unaware of the underlying motives for his or her behavior. (p. 211)

18. c. a psychological defense involving a slitting-off of consciousness to block out unacceptable memories or impulses. (p. 205)

19. d. selective amnesia (p. 200)

20. a. involves no memory disturbance. (pp. 203, 204)

21. a. quite suddenly. (p. 201)

22. c. trauma (p. 206)

23. d. all of the above. (p. 218)

24. c. shy and introverted. (p. 207)

25. d. finding yourself in a place and not knowing how you got there. (p. 203)

26. a. factitious disorder. (p. 211)

27. a. the individual consciously fakes their symptoms. (p. 211)

28. d. relieve anxiety. (pp. 217-218)

29. a. self-handicapping strategy. (p. 218)

30. b. relieve anxiety. (p. 218)

ANSWERS TO SHORT ANSWER QUESTIONS

1. Dissociative disorders are characterized by a disruption or dissociation of identity, memory, or consciousness. The major dissociative disorders include dissociative identity disorder, dissociative amnesia, dissociative fugue, and depersonalization disorder. Dissociative identity disorder involves the emergence of two or more distinct personalities. Alternative personalities may display different EEG recordings, have different allergic reactions, and different responses to medication. Alternate personalities may also vie for control. Dissociative amnesia is characterized by an inability to recall important personal material and cannot be accounted for by medical causes. Localized amnesia (events occurring during a specific time period are lost to memory), selective amnesia (disturbing specifics of a certain time period are lost to memory), and generalized amnesia (total memory loss of a person's life) are subtypes of dissociative amnesia. Dissociative fugue is amnesia 'on the run.' Individuals with this disorder travel to a new location and are unable to remember personal information. Individuals may also begin new lives with new identities. Depersonalization disorder involves episodes of feelings of detachment from one's self or one's body or having a sense of derealization. These experiences may cause significant distress for the individual. (pp. 195-204)

2. Somatoform disorders are characterized by physical complaints that cannot be accounted for by medical causes. The major somatoform disorders include conversion disorder, hypochondriasis, somatization disorder, and body dysmorphic disorder. Conversion disorder involves a change or loss of a physical function without organic cause. This disorder often emerges within a context of conflict and stress and may be associated with 'la belle indifference.' An individual with conversion disorder is does not intentionally produce symptoms and is therefore not malingering. Hypochodriasis is characterized by a preoccupation with the belief one is seriously ill. Unlike conversion disorder, hypochondriasis does not involve the loss or distortion of physical function. An individual with this disorder is very concerned about symptoms and may be fearful of what they represent. Somatization disorder involves recurrent, multiple complains about physical symptoms that have no medical cause. Complaints often prompt frequent medical visits or cause significant impairment in functioning. Body dysmorphic disorder is characterized by a preoccupation with an imagined or exaggerated physical defect. An individual with this disorder may engage in compulsive behaviors in an attempt to remedy the perceived defect. (pp. 211-215)

3. Dissociative and somatoform disorders were once grouped together with anxiety disorders in early versions of the DSM. This common grouping was based upon the psychodynamic model. The role of anxiety in dissociative and somatoform disorders was inferred. Individuals with these disorders may not display overt signs of anxiety but may display symptoms that (according to the psychodynamic model) serve to keep underlying sources of anxiety out of awareness. The current version of the DSM separates anxiety disorders from dissociative and somatoform disorders. (p. 195)

4. The diagnosis of dissociative identity disorder is a controversial one. Some professional believe that the increased number of diagnosed cases in recent years reflects underreporting in earlier time periods. Others believe that dissociative identity disorder is over diagnosed in highly suggestible individuals and increased public attention may account for the increased number of reported cases. Dissociative identity disorder appears to be culture bound, largely restricted to North America. Critics of the diagnosis believe that multiple personality represents a form of role playing, and with proper cues, a person may easily enact this role. Clinicians may unknowingly cue clients to enact the multiple personality role and reinforce the performance with attention and concern. (pp. 198-199)

5. Childhood sexual abuse plays a pivotal role in the etiology of dissociative disorders. A popular view of dissociative identity disorder is that it represents a means of coping with, and surviving, severe childhood abuse. The abused child may retreat into an alternate personality as a psychological defense against the abuse. The majority of individuals with multiple personalities report being physically or sexually abused in childhood. In one study, eighty three percent of individuals with dissociative identity disorder reported a history of childhood sexual abuse. (p. 206)

ANSWERS TO CROSSWORD

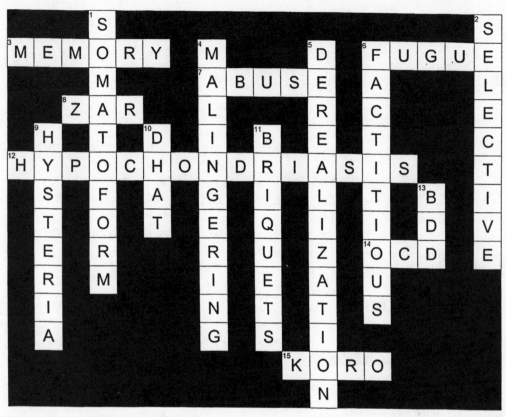

ACROSS	DOWN
3. a reconstructive process	1. disorders involving physical symptoms without an organic basis
6. 'flight'	2. amnesia for specific details of an event
7. plays pivotal role in etiology of multiple personality	4. deliberately faking symptoms
8. spirit possession in those who experience dissociative states	5. changes in the perceptions of one's surroundings or time
12. abnormal fear that physical symptom is result of serious underlying illness	6. disorder involving fabrication of symptoms with no apparent goal
14. linked with BDD	9. now referred to as conversion disorder
15. fear that genitals are shrinking	10. fears over loss of seminal fluid
	11. now known as somatization disorder
	13. preoccupation with an imagined physical defect

ACROSS
3. a reconstructive process
6. 'flight'
7. plays pivotal role in etiology of multiple personality
8. spirit possession in those who experience dissociative states
12. abnormal fear that physical symptom is result of serious underlying illness
14. linked with BDD
15. fear that genitals are shrinking

DOWN
1. disorders involving physical symptoms without an organic basis
2. amnesia for specific details of an event
4. deliberately faking symptoms
5. changes in the perceptions of one's surroundings or time
6. disorder involving fabrication of symptoms with no apparent goal
9. now referred to as conversion disorder
10. fears over loss of seminal fluid
11. now known as somatization disorder
13. preoccupation with an imagined physical defect

CHAPTER EIGHT

MOOD DISORDERS AND SUICIDE

OBJECTIVES

1. Describe the features of major depressive disorder and dysthymic disorder and distinguish between them.
2. Discuss the prevalence of major depressive disorder, with particular attention to ethnic and gender risk factors.
3. Discuss seasonal affective disorder and postpartum depression.
4. Describe the features of bipolar disorder and cyclothymic disorder and distinguish between them.
5. Discuss the relationship between stress and mood disorders.
6. Discuss the psychodynamic, humanistic, learning, cognitive, and biological perspectives on the origins and treatment of mood disorders.
7. Discuss the incidence of suicide and theoretical perspectives on its causes.

CHAPTER OUTLINE

Types of Mood Disorders
      Major Depressive Disorder
      Dysthymic Disorder
      Bipolar Disorder
      Cyclothymic Disorder
Theoretical Perspectives on Mood Disorders
      Stress and Mood Disorders
      Psychodynamic Theories
      Humanistic Theories
      Learning Theories
      Cognitive Theories
      Cognitive Theories
      Biological Factors
      Tying It Together
Treatment of Mood Disorders
      Psychodynamic Approaches
      Behavioral Approaches
      Cognitive Approaches
      Biological Approaches
      Clinical practice Guidelines for Depression
Suicide
      Who Commits Suicide?
      Why Do People Commit Suicide
      Theoretical Perspectives on Suicide
      Predicting Suicide
Summing Up

MATCHING

Answers are found at the end of this chapter. Match these terms and concepts with the definitions that follow:

Peter Lewinsohn
ambivalence
bereavement
St. John's Wort
dysthymia
introject
hypersomnia
automatic thoughts
phototherapy
humanistic theory
cyclothymia
tricyclics
reformulated helplessness theory
moods
SAD
cognitive triad of depression
bipolar
selective abstraction
learned helplessness
anomie

hypomanic episodes
rapid cycling
cognitive-specificity hypothesis
Interactional theory
Martin Seligman
postpartum depression
cognitive therapy
SSRIs
psychodynamic theory
ruminating
cognitive distortions
double depression
Coping with Depression Course
unipolar
bipolar disorder
mood disorder
self-focusing model
ECT
lithium carbonate
major depressive disorder

1._____ habitual thoughts that are accepted without analysis as facts

2._____ major depressive episode superimposed on an episode of dysthymia

3._____ persistent depressed mood following childbirth

4._____ oversleeping; a symptom of major depression

5._____ women, more often than men, amplify depression by doing this

6._____ increase levels of norepinephrine and serotonin by interfering with their reuptake in the brain

7._____ long periods of mildly elevated or depressed mood

8._____ individual experiences two or more full cycles of mania and depression within a year

9._____ normal reaction to the death of another person

10._____ this theory suggests that depression is due to anger turned inward against the self

11._____ simultaneously experienced strongly negative and strongly positive feelings

12._____ this theory suggests that depression develops when people do not find their lives meaningful and cannot make authentic choices leading to self-fulfillment

13._____ a treatment for seasonal depression consisting of daily exposure to bright light

14._____ this theory suggests that acting depressed elicits subtle negative reactions from significant others

15._____ periods of elevated mood with less severe symptoms and impairment than manic episodes

16._____ mild, but persistent depression for at least two years

17._____ "bringing inward" a mental representation

18._____ an herb that may increase the levels of serotonin in the brain by interfering with its reabsorption

19._____ treatment of depression, which focuses on identifying distorted thoughts and substituting rational ones

20._____ this theory posits that different disorders are characterized by different automatic thoughts

21._____ behavioral treatment of depression emphasizing relaxation, pleasant activities, and social skills

22._____ developed the learned helplessness theory of depression, later reformulating this theory using the concept of attributional style

23._____ errors in thinking that theoretically set the stage for depression in the face of negative life events

24._____ developed a behavioral theory of depression, emphasizing lack of reinforcement in the environment

25._____ the theory that depression is due to the types of attributions a person makes

26._____ increase levels of serotonin in the brain by interfering with their reuptake

27._____ enduring states of feeling

28._____ pertaining to a single direction

29. _____ a type of depression related to changes in season

30. _____ a disorder characterized by mood swings between states of extreme elation and depression

31. _____ a view that depression results from adopting negative views of oneself, the world, and the future

32. _____ a disorder characterized by disturbance in mood

33. _____ pertaining to two directions; characterized by opposite ends of a dimension

34. _____ a model that considers how individuals allocate their attentional processes after a loss

35. _____ a cognitive distortion in which the individual focuses on only the negative parts of experiences

36. _____ a treatment method for depression that involves the administration of an electric current to the head

37. _____ a behavior pattern characterized by passivity and a perceived lack of control

38. _____ medication used to treat bipolar disorder

39. _____ a feeling of rootlessness

40. _____ also called major depression

CROSSWORD

Answers are found at the end of this chapter. Complete the following crossword puzzle to reinforce your understanding of this chapter's key terms and concepts:

ACROSS		DOWN	
2. experiencing negative and positive emotions simultaneously	14. habitual thoughts accepted without analysis	1. periods of elevated moods less severe than manic episodes	11. treatment that focuses on thinking patterns
4. treatment for seasonal depression	15. used to treat bipolar disorder	3. theory focusing on reactions from significant others	13. major depression in response to specific loss
5. normal reaction to death of another	16. mild but persistent depression	7. increase levels of norepinephrine	
6. long periods of mildly elevated or depressed moods	17. feeling of rootlessness	8. enduring states of feeling	
9. pertaining to two directions	18. developed learned helplessness theory	10. type of depression related to changes in season	
12. increase levels of serotonin by blocking reuptake			

MULTIPLE CHOICE

Answers are found at the end of this chapter. The multiple choice questions listed will test your understanding of the material presented in the chapter. Read through each question and circle the letter representing the best answer.

1. Which of the following is typical of a person experiencing normal feelings of sadness as compared to someone who is clinically depressed?
    a. feelings of depressed mood that pass quickly
    b. large decrease in physical activity
    c. recurrent thoughts of suicide
    d. faulty perceptions of reality

2. Which of the following groups has the highest rate of depression?
    a. married men
    b. married women
    c. women who have never been married
    d. men who have recently been divorced

3. MAO inhibitors
    a. block the activity of an enzyme.
    b. stimulate release of neurotransmitters.
    c. inhibit reuptake sites on postsynaptic membranes.
    d. are more effective drugs than tricyclics for depression.

4. Which of the following types of delusions would be most likely to be found in depression?
    a. delusions of persecution ("Somebody is out to get me.")
    b. delusions of grandeur ("I am the reincarnation of Buddha.")
    c. delusions of reference ("The book on display with the title Making Your Will is a message that I am going to die this week.")
    d. delusions of unworthiness or guilt ("I have committed a terrible crime.")

5. Which of the following is a diagnostic feature of major depression?
    a. shortness of breath
    b. rapid flight of ideas
    c. persistent inability to sleep
    d. repetitive and stereotyped motor activity

6. The tendency to "make mountains out of molehills" is referred to as
    a. catastrophizing or magnification.
    b. mental filtering.
    c. overgeneralization.
    d. musterbation.

7. Which of the following statements is not considered a possible explanation for the higher rate of depression in women?
    a. greater stressful life events such as abuse, poverty, and sexism
    b. hormonal changes
    c. greater social support
    d. difference in coping styles

8. Interpersonal therapy for depression differs from traditional psychodynamic treatments in that
    a. interpersonal therapy focuses on the clients' current relationships.
    b. interpersonal therapy focuses on early childhood experiences.
    c. interpersonal therapy focuses on conflicts between the ego and the superego.
    d. interpersonal therapy focuses on establishing goals for the future.

9. Research on the self-focusing model of depression suggests that
    a. depressed persons typically do not focus on themselves but on other people.
    b. depressed persons focus on themselves more than others following successes.
    c. self-focused attention has been linked to disorders other than depression.
    d. self-focused attention in depressed people is lower following failures.

10. People who experience a repeated pattern of severe fall and winter depression may be diagnosed with
    a. endogenous depression.
    b. seasonal affective disorder.
    c. cyclothymia.
    d. reactive depression.

11. Which of the following statements is true regarding treatment for depression?
    a. Psychological treatments are more effective in treating people with severe depression than antidepressant medication.
    b. People who do not respond to antidepressant medication are not likely to benefit from psychotherapy.
    c. A combination of one of the recommended forms of psychotherapy and antidepressant medication may be an effective approach in treating depression.
    d. Over the long run, antidepressant medication is more cost-effective than psychotherapy.

12. Lithium as a treatment of bipolar disorder
    a. is extremely safe with few side effects.
    b. has clearly understood pharmacological effects.
    c. can be discontinued once normal mood is established.
    d. is the most widely used drug for treatment of manic episodes.

13. If you think you are dealing with a person who is considering committing suicide, which of the following statements would be the best response?
   a. "You're talking crazy."
   b. "Let's wait and see how you feel next week."
   c. "Come with me and we'll find some help."
   d. "Everyone feels that way sometimes."

14. SSRI's have largely replaced tricyclic drugs for treatment for depression because
   a. they are more cost-effective.
   b. they do not have the same delayed effect as tricyclics, rather, people respond within 24 hours.
   c. they are much more effective in the treatment of depression.
   d. they are less toxic and have fewer side effects.

15. Which of the following group is at greatest risk for suicide?
   a. non-Hispanic white youth
   b. Native-American youth
   c. African-American youth
   d. Asian-American youth

16. Which of the following is not one of the characteristics of a manic episode?
   a. pressured speech
   b. psychomotor retardation
   c. decreased need for sleep
   d. impaired social judgment

17. A person who experiences one episode of major depression
   a. is unlikely to have another episode for at least two years.
   b. is likely to have another episode.
   c. if left untreated, will never completely recover.
   d. is more likely to develop a psychotic disorder than a person who has never had a depressive episode.

18. According to the guidelines issued by an expert panel in 1993, which of the following treatments have been shown to be effective for the treatment of depression?
   a. antidepressant medication
   b. cognitive therapy, behavior therapy, and interpersonal therapy
   c. other specified treatments such as ECT
   d. all of the above

19. Which of the following best describes the differences between bipolar disorder and cyclothymia?
   a. impairment in cyclothymic individuals is much greater.
   b. the age of onset in cyclothymia is later than in bipolar disorder.
   c. the hypomanic episodes in cyclothymia are less severe than manic episodes in bipolar disorder.
   d. cyclothymic individuals can have periods of normal mood lasting as long as six months.

20. Which of the following may act as a buffer against the onset of depression during stressful times?
     a. social support
     b. having the same job for several years
     c. living alone
     d. having a college degree

21. Which of the following is not part of the cognitive triad of depression?
     a. negative beliefs about oneself
     b. negative beliefs about the environment
     c. negative beliefs about the past
     d. negative beliefs about the future

22. Which of the following is one way that dysthymia differs from major depression?
     a. major depression lasts longer than dysthymia.
     b. dysthymia is characterized by rapid cycling of moods.
     c. major depression functions as part of a person's personality.
     d. dysthymia tends to develop earlier and more gradually.

23. The three types of attributions most vulnerable to depression are
     a. external, global, and unstable attributions.
     b. external, specific, and unstable attributions.
     c. internal, specific, and stable attributions.
     d. internal, global, and stable attributions.

24. Investigators have found evidence of lower metabolic activity in this area of clinically depressed individuals as compared to healthy controls:
     a. prefrontal cortex.
     b. temporal lobe.
     c. somatosensory cortex.
     d. visual cortex.

25. Research on the relationship between cognitions and depression supports that
     a. the relationship may depend more on the balance between negative and positive thoughts than the presence of negative thoughts alone.
     b. there is a causal relationship between negative cognitions and onset of depression.
     c. people who are not depressed rarely experience negative thoughts.
     d. distorted cognitions are extremely resistant to treatment.

26. Cognitive therapy seeks to help clients recognize cognitive distortions. Which of the following is an example of a cognitive distortion?
     a. "I know I'm going to flunk this course."
     b. "Stop blaming yourself for everyone else's problems."
     c. "Feeling something doesn't make it so."
     d. "Nobody is destined to be a loser."

27. Which theory of suicide suggests and emphasizes that people committing suicide do so because they may be motivated by positive expectancies and approving attitudes toward suicide?
   a. psychodynamic theory
   b. social-cognitive theory
   c. interpersonal theory
   d. humanistic-existential theory

28. Major depression affects how many adults?
   a. approximately one in one hundred
   b. nearly one in twenty
   c. nearly one in five
   d. almost one-half of the adult population

29. MZ twins show _____ concordance for major depression and _____ concordance for bipolar disorder than DZ twins.
   a. higher; higher
   b. higher, lower
   c. lower; higher
   d. lower; lower

30. Among which age group are suicide rates the highest?
   a. children
   b. adolescents
   c. mature adults
   d. elderly

SHORT ANSWER

Answers are found at the end of this chapter. Answer the following short answer questions:

1. How do clinicians distinguish between normal and abnormal variations in moods?
2. List and describe the major types of mood disorders.
3. What is the difference between unipolar disorders and bipolar disorders?
4. How do clinicians distinguish between a manic episode and a hypomanic episode?
5. What are the features of seasonal affective disorder and postpartum depression?

VIDEO/CD-ROM

In order to obtain greater insight into the information presented in this chapter, refer to the videos that accompany it.

Video 8.1   Depression: The Case of Helen
Video 8.2   Bipolar Disorder: The Case of Craig

ANSWERS TO MATCHING

1. automatic thoughts (p. 244)

2. double depression (p. 232)

3. postpartum depression (p. 230)

4. hypersomnia (p. 227)

5. ruminating (p. 229)

6. tricyclics (p. 255)

7. cyclothymia (p. 235)

8. rapid cycling (p. 233)

9. bereavement (p. 227)

10. psychodynamic theory (p. 237)

11. ambivalence (p. 237)

12. humanistic theory (p. 239)

13. phototherapy (p. 230)

14. interactional theory (pp. 240-241)

15. hypomanic episodes (p. 226)

16. dysthymia (p. 231)

17. introject (p. 238)

18. St. John's Wort (p. 256)

19. cognitive therapy (p. 252)

20. cognitive specificity hypothesis (p. 244)

21. Coping with Depression Course (p. 252)

22. Martin Seligman (pp. 246, 247)

23. cognitive distortions (p. 242)

24. Peter Lewinsohn (pp. 239-240)

25. reformulated helplessness theory (p. 247)

26. SSRIs (p. 255)

27. moods (p. 225)

28. unipolar (p. 226)

29. SAD (p. 229)

30. bipolar disorder (p. 233)

31. cognitive triad of depression (p. 241)

32. mood disorder (p. 225)

33. bipolar (p. 226)

34. self-focusing model (p. 238)

35. selective abstraction (p. 242)

36. ECT (p. 257)

37. learned helplessness (pp. 246, 247)

38. lithium carbonate (p. 256)

39. anomie (p. 361)

40. major depressive disorder (p. 226)

ANSWERS TO MULTIPLE CHOICE QUESTIONS

1. a. feelings of depressed mood that pass quickly (p. 226)

2. d. men who have recently been divorced (p. 228)

3. c. inhibit reuptake sites on postsynaptic membranes. (p. 255)

4. d. delusions of unworthiness or guilt ("I have committed a terrible crime.") (p. 227)

5. c. persistent inability to sleep (p. 227)

6. a catastrophizing or magnification. (p. 243)

7. c. greater social support (p. 250)

8. a. interpersonal therapy focuses on the client's current relationships. (p. 251)

9. c. self-focused attention has been linked to disorders other than depression. (p. 238)

10. b. seasonal affective disorder. (p. 229)

11. c. A combination of one of the recommended forms of psychotherapy and antidepressant medication may be an effective approach in treating depression. (p. 258)

12. d. is the most widely used drug for treatment of manic episodes. (pp. 256-257)

13. c. "Come with me, and we'll find some help." (p. 263)

14. d. they are less toxic and have fewer side effects. (p. 255)

15. b. Native American youth (pp. 259, 260)

16. b. psychomotor retardation (pp. 233-234)

17. b. is likely to have another episode. (p. 228)

18. d. all of the above (p. 258)

19. c. the hypomanic episodes in cyclothymia are less severe than manic episodes in bipolar disorder. (p. 235)

20. a. social support (p. 236)

21. c. negative beliefs about the past (p. 242)

22. d. dysthymia tends to develop earlier and more gradually. (pp. 231, 232)

23. d. internal, global, and stable attributions. (p. 247)

24. a. prefrontal cortex (p. 249)

25. a. the relationship may depend more on the balance between negative and positive thoughts than the presence of negative thoughts alone. (p. 245)

26. a. "I know I'm going to flunk this course." (pp. 242, 243)

27. b. social-cognitive theory (p. 262)

28. c. nearly one in five (p. 227)

29. a. higher; higher (p. 248)

30. d. elderly (p. 258)

ANSWERS TO SHORT ANSWER QUESTIONS

1. What is considered normal or abnormal is largely based upon context. Feeling depressed in the context of depressing circumstances is not abnormal. However, if disturbances of mood are unusually severe and impair an individual's ability to function, one may be diagnosed with a mood disorder. (p. 225)

2. Mood disorders are characterized by disturbances of mood or emotion. Included are major depressive disorder, dysthymic disorder, bipolar disorder, and cyclothymia. Major depressive disorder involves episodes of severe depression. An individual with major depressive disorder may display a range of symptoms, including downcast mood, feelings of helplessness and hopelessness, and appetite and sleep disturbance. Dysthymic disorder is a pattern of mild depression that lasts for an extended period of time (several years). Individuals may suffer from 'double depression,' whereby a major depressive episode is superimposed upon a longer standing dysthymic condition. Bipolar disorder is characterized by mood swings, ranging from elation (mania) to depression. There are two general types of bipolar disorder. Bipolar I disorder involves at least one full manic episode. A manic episode includes a period of unrealistically heightened euphoria, extreme restlessness, disorganized behavior, and impaired judgment. Bipolar II disorder is associated with a milder form of mania. An individual with this disorder experiences one or more major depressive episodes and at least one hypomanic episode. Cyclothymic disorder is characterized by a chronic pattern of mild mood swings that is not sufficiently severe to be classified as bipolar disorder. The individual with cyclothymia experiences cyclical patterns of shifting mood states from hypomanic episodes to states of mild depression. (pp. 226-235)

3. The term 'unipolar' pertains to a single pole or direction, whereas 'bipolar' refers to opposite ends of a continuum. The depressive disorders are considered unipolar because disturbances in mood lie in only one emotional direction:down. Disorders characterized by mood swings are bipolar as they involve both depression and elation, usually in an alternating pattern. (pp. 225, 226).

4. Manic episodes are characterized by periods of unrealistically heightened euphoria, extreme restlessness, disorganized behavior, and impaired judgment. People in a manic episode display pressured speech, whereby words seem to surge for expression. A rapid flight of ideas is also characteristic of a manic episode in which the individual's thoughts and speech may jump from topic to topic. Hypomanic episodes are less severe than manic episodes and are not accompanied by severe social problems associated with full-blown manic episodes. Hypomanic episodes are characterized by elevated moods. During hypomanic episodes, individuals may have an inflated sense of self, high energy, and experience restlessness. Behavior does not become as disorganized and judgment is not as impaired as what is witnessed in a manic episode. (pp. 233-235)

5. Seasonal affective disorder (SAD) is a type of depression characterized by fatigue, excessive sleep, craving for carbohydrates, and weight gain. Although the exact etiology is unknown, it is possible that seasonal changes in light may change the body's underlying biological rhythms that regulate body temperature, one's sleep/wake cycle, and serotonin production. Postpartum depression (PPD) involves persistent and severe mood changes that occur after childbirth. Symptoms include disturbances in appetite and sleep, low self-esteem, and difficulties concentrating. Etiological factors include chemical imbalances (neurotransmitters and hormones) and environmental stressors. (pp. 229-231)

ANSWERS TO CROSSWORD

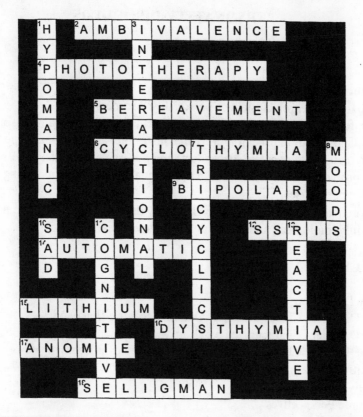

ACROSS		DOWN	
2. experiencing negative and positive emotions simultaneously	14. habitual thoughts accepted without analysis	1. periods of elevated moods less severe than manic episodes	11. treatment that focuses on thinking patterns
4. treatment for seasonal depression	15. used to treat bipolar disorder	3. theory focusing on reactions from significant others	13. major depression in response to specific loss
5. normal reaction to death of another	16. mild but persistent depression	7. increase levels of norepinephrine	
6. long periods of mildly elevated or depressed moods	17. feeling of rootlessness	8. enduring states of feeling	
9. pertaining to two directions	18. developed learned helplessness theory	10. type of depression related to changes in season	
12. increase levels of serotonin by blocking reuptake			

CHAPTER NINE

PERSONALITY DISORDERS

OBJECTIVES

1. Define personality disorder.
2. Describe the three research clusters of personality disorders.
3. Describe the features of paranoid, schizoid, and schizotypal personality disorders.
4. Describe the features of antisocial, borderline, histrionic, and narcissistic personality disorders.
5. Describe the features of avoidant, dependent, and obsessive-compulsive personality disorders.
6. Discuss the problems in the classification of personality disorders, including their reliability, validity, and sexist biases.
7. Discuss theoretical perspectives on the personality disorders, including the psychodynamic, learning, family, biological, and sociocultural perspectives.

CHAPTER OUTLINE

Types of Personality Disorders
      Personality Disorders Characterized by Odd or Eccentric Behavior
      Personality Disorders Characterized by Dramatic, Emotional, or Erratic Behavior
      Personality Disorders Characterized by Anxious or Fearful Behavior
      Problems with the Classification of Personality Disorders
Theoretical Perspectives
      Psychodynamic Perspectives
      Learning Perspectives
      Family Perspectives
      Biological Perspectives
      Sociocultural Perspectives
Treatment of Personality Disorders
      Psychodynamic Approaches
      Behavioral Approaches
      Biological Approaches
Summing Up

MATCHING

Answers are found at the end of this chapter. Match these terms and concepts with the definitions that follow:

Hans Kohut	dialectical behavior therapy
splitting	Margaret Mahler
Cluster C: anxious or fearful	instability of moods
ego-dystonic	rejection
token economies	Ullman and Krasner
Hervey Cleckley	problem-solving therapy

separation-individuation
abandonment
Cluster A: odd or eccentric
sociopath
"healthful narcissism"
males
optimum level of arousal
schizoid personality disorder
paranoid personality disorder
BPD
self-mutilation
schizotypal personality disorder
avoidant personality disorder
self-psychology

ego-syntonic
Cluster B: dramatic or erratic
circular reasoning
females
social phobia
ideas of reference
symbiosis
personality disorders
histrionic personality disorder
behavioral dimension
obsessive-compulsive personality disorder
personality dimension
dependent personality disorder
antisocial personality disorder

1._____ individuals with avoidant personality disorder are terrified of this

2._____ perception that feelings and behavior are foreign to one's self-identity

3._____ fleeting beliefs that other people are taking special notice about you or talking about you behind your back

4._____ psychodynamic theorist(s) who related narcissistic personality disorder to lack of parental empathy and support

5._____ a term describing antisocial behavior that centers on a person's social deviance

6._____ a treatment approach for borderline personality disorder combining behavior and supportive therapy

7._____ reasoning that confuses diagnostic labeling with explanation

8._____ individuals with borderline personality disorder cannot tolerate this

9._____ central characteristic of borderline personality disorder

10._____ antisocial, borderline, histrionic, and narcissistic personality disorders

11._____ used in residential programs to reward behaviors that are targeted for development

12._____ a degree of arousal at which people feel best and function most efficiently

13._____ psychodynamic theorist(s) who related borderline personality disorders to childhood separation from mother figure

14. _____ a treatment for antisocial boys that emphasizes reconceptualizing social interactions as problems to be solved

15. _____ learning perspective theorist(s) who proposed that antisocial personality disorders are failure to respond to social reinforcers

16. _____ wrote "The Mask of Sanity," describing antisocial personality features

17. _____ a psychological term that describes the state of oneness in which a child's identity is fused with the mother's identity

18. _____ paranoid, schizoid, and schizotypal personality disorders

19. _____ histrionic personality disorder is diagnosed more frequently in this group

20. _____ there is a good deal of overlap between this and avoidant personality disorder

21. _____ antisocial personality disorder is more than five times as common among this group than the other

22. _____ a psychodynamic term that describes the shifting back and forth between viewing oneself or others as "all good" or "all bad"

23. _____ avoidant, dependent, and obsessive-compulsive personality disorders

24. _____ the process of developing a separate psychological and biological identity from the mother and recognizing the defining characteristics of one's own identity

25. _____ according to Kohut, a stage of normal development in early childhood when infants feel powerful and believe that the world revolves around them

26. _____ perception that behavior and one's feelings are a natural part of one's self

27. _____ excessively rigid behavior patterns that ultimately become self-defeating

28. _____ a personality disorder characterized by suspiciousness of others' motives

29. _____ a personality disorder characterized by excessive need for approval, attention, praise, and reassurance

30. _____ a dimension of the psychopathic personality characterized by the adoption of a generally unstable and antisocial lifestyle

31. _____ a personality disorder characterized by rigid ways of relating to others, perfectionistic tendencies, lack of spontaneity, and attention to detail

32. _____ a theory that describes processes which normally lead to achievement of a cohesive sense of self

33. _____ a personality disorder characterized by antisocial and irresponsible behavior and lack of remorse

34. _____ a personality disorder characterized by overly dependent behavior and difficulty making independent decisions

35. _____ a personality disorder characterized by avoidance of social relationships for fear of rejection

36. _____ a dimension of the psychopathic personality characterized by traits such as superficial charm, selfishness, and lack of empathy

37. _____ sometimes carried out as an expression of anger by those with BPD

38. _____ a personality disorder characterized by eccentricities of thought and behavior, but without clear psychotic features

39. _____ a personality disorder characterized by abrupt shifts in mood, lack of a coherent sense of self, and impulsive behavior

40. _____ a personality disorder characterized by persistent lack of interest in social relationships, flattened affect, and social withdrawal

CROSSWORD

Answers are found at the end of this chapter. Complete the following crossword puzzle to reinforce your understanding of this chapter's key terms and concepts:

ACROSS	DOWN
2. perceiving one's feelings as foreign to one's identity	1. repeating same action over and over again
3. perceiving one's feelings as natural part of one's self	4. personality disorder characterized by excessive need for approval
5. antisocial, borderline, histrionic disorders	6. viewing others as 'all good' or 'all bad'
8. personality disorder characterized by antisocial behavior	7. level of arousal at which people feel their best
10. characterized by abrupt shifts in mood and impulsiveness	9. state of oneness between child and mother
12. avoidant, dependent, and obsessive-compulsive disorders	11. paranoid, schizoid, schizotypal disorders
13. reasoning that confuses labeling with explanation	

MULTIPLE CHOICE

Answers are found at the end of this chapter. The multiple choice questions listed will test your understanding of the material presented in the chapter. Read through each question and circle the letter representing the best answer.

1. The term "borderline" was originally used to describe
   a. people whose behaviors appeared to border between sane and insane.
   b. people whose behaviors appeared to border between schizophrenic and manic.
   c. people whose behaviors appeared to border between neurotic and psychotic.
   d. people whose behaviors appeared to border between depressed and antisocial.

2. Which of these is not part of Cleckley's clinical profile of antisocial personality disorder?
   a. responding to setbacks with depression or fury
   b. lack of remorse or shame
   c. inability to profit from experience
   d. superficial charm and intelligence

3. About _____ people with personality disorders meet diagnostic criteria for more than one personality disorder.
   a. one in ten
   b. one in four
   c. two in three
   d. one in two

4. Which is not an example of self-defeating narcissism?
   a. responding to life's wounds with depression or fury
   b. feeling entitled to special treatment and becoming very upset when treated in an ordinary manner
   c. being temporarily wounded by criticism
   d. needing constant support from other people in order to feel good about oneself

5. Extreme focus on details, rigidity in relationships, limited ability to express feelings, and difficulty relaxing and having fun are characteristic of
   a. schizoid personality disorder.
   b. obsessive-compulsive personality disorder.
   c. dependent personality disorder.
   d. borderline personality disorder.

6. In all but which one of the following personality disorders would you expect the individuals to be loners?
   a. avoidant
   b. schizoid
   c. histrionic
   d. schizotypal

7. The relatives of probands with _____ are more likely to be diagnosed as suffering from a schizophrenia-spectrum disorder.
    a. schizoid personality disorder
    b. paranoid personality disorder
    c. schizotypal personality disorder
    d. borderline personality disorder

8. Analogy: fear of rejection is to lack of interest in social relations as
    a. dependent personality disorder is to schizotypal personality disorder.
    b. schizotypal personality disorder is to avoidant personality disorder.
    c. avoidant personality disorder is to schizoid personality disorder.
    d. schizoid personality disorder is to avoidant personality disorder.

9. The dialectical behavior therapy approach in treating BPD involves
    a. behavior therapy and supportive therapy.
    b. supportive therapy.
    c. relaxation therapy.
    d. systematic desensitization.

10. A commonality of learning theory and psychodynamic theory in explaining the development of personality disorders is the
    a. genetic history of the individual.
    b. physical abnormalities present at birth.
    c. the person's ability to develop a strong sense of identity.
    d. salient childhood experiences.

11. What personality disorder has been used most to explain the concept of self?
    a. narcissistic
    b. antisocial
    c. dependent
    d. histrionic

12. In which personality disorder does the person find it difficult to do things on his or her own?
    a. dependent personality disorder
    b. avoidant personality disorder
    c. obsessive-compulsive personality disorder
    d. antisocial personality disorder

13. In their explanation of the origins of personality disorders, which stage of development have the more recent psychodynamic theories focused on?
    a. infancy
    b. preoedipal stage
    c. oedipal stage
    d. latency stage

14. Which is not found in studies of antisocial personality?
    a. ability to learn from experience
    b. high sensation seeking
    c. under-responsive nervous system
    d. brain abnormalities

15. Narcissistic personality disorder is most known for
    a. disregard for the law.
    b. uncertain values.
    c. inflated sense of self.
    d. social isolation.

16. With which personality disorder would an individual be most likely to use splitting?
    a. narcissistic personality disorder
    b. borderline personality disorder
    c. dependent personality disorder
    d. avoidant personality disorder

17. Which of the following personality disorders is more commonly diagnosed in females?
    a. antisocial personality disorder
    b. schizoid personality disorder
    c. paranoid personality disorder
    d. borderline personality disorder

18. Which personality disorder seems to be a caricature of the feminine personality?
    a. histrionic personality disorder
    b. avoidant personality disorder
    c. obsessive-compulsive personality disorder
    d. schizoid personality disorder

19. For persons under the age of eighteen, an appropriate diagnosis to consider for antisocial behavior is
    a. antisocial personality disorder.
    b. schizoid personality disorder.
    c. conduct disorder.
    d. adjustment disorder.

20. Which personality disorder name derives from Latin for actor?
    a. histrionic
    b. narcissistic
    c. schizoid
    d. paranoid

21. One problem with labeling people with disturbing behavior as having a personality disorder is that
    a. it lacks validity and reliability.
    b. the social and environmental contexts in which the behavior occurs is overlooked.
    c. behavior is inconsistent across time.
    d. the focus on the role of traumatic life events in shaping behavior is too heavily emphasized.

22. Which of the following statements is true regarding treatment of personality disorders?
    a. people with personality disorders do not usually seek treatment on their own.
    b. people with personality disorders often drop out of treatment prematurely.
    c. people who seek treatment for disorders such as depression and who also have personality disorders often respond poorly to treatment.
    d. all of the above.

23. The role of observational learning in aggressive behavior, a component of antisocial behavior was emphasized by
    a. Ullman and Krasner.
    b. Mary Ainsworth.
    c. Albert Bandura.
    d. Otto Kernberg.

24. Researchers have begun to conceptualize psychopathic personality as composed of two, somewhat independent dimensions. They include
    a. a cognitive dimension and a social dimension.
    b. a symptom dimension and a personality dimension.
    c. a personality dimension and a behavioral dimension.
    d. a cognitive dimension and a behavioral dimension.

25. People who may appear to be guarded or suspicious might be
    a. diagnosed with schizoid personality disorder.
    b. experiencing ego-dystonic symptoms.
    c. unfamiliar with the customs and rules of the majority culture.
    d. planning to commit a crime.

26. Antisocial personality disorder is more common among
    a. people from lower SES levels.
    b. Hispanic-Americans.
    c. African-Americans.
    d. people with childhood psychiatric problems.

27. Failure to develop a coherent self image is a key sign of
    a. borderline personality disorder.
    b. antisocial personality disorder.
    c. histrionic personality disorder.
    d. narcissistic personality disorder.

28. Which of the following statements best summarizes the role of genetic factors in personality disorders?
    a. Research has demonstrated direct evidence of genetic transmission of personality disorders.
    b. Research suggest genetic factors play a role in the development of certain personality disorders.
    c. The only personality dimension that may have an inherited component is lack of emotional responsivity.
    d. Research has supported that the development of all personality disorders is completely due to environmental factors.

29. Which of the following is not a factor related to sensation seeking?
    a. pursuit of thrill and adventure
    b. susceptibility to boredom
    c. pursuit of experience
    d. inhibition

30. Which of the following is not a major controversy in the classification of personality disorders?
    a. too many cases that fit two or more diagnostic categories
    b. excessive ambiguity in diagnostic criteria
    c. inclusion of traits that are normal in lesser degree as key diagnostic criteria
    d. debate as to whether personality disorders need a separate axis in DSM or should be included in Axis I

SHORT ANSWER

Answers are found at the end of this chapter. Answer the following short answer questions:

1. What are personality disorders? How are they classified in the DSM system?
2. List and describe Cluster A personality disorders.
3. List and describe Cluster B personality disorders.
4. List and describe Cluster C personality disorders.
5. Discuss the problems with the classification of personality disorders.

VIDEO/CD-ROM

In order to obtain greater insight into the information presented in this chapter, refer to the video that accompanies it.

Video 9.1   Antisocial Personality Disorder: The Case of Paul

ANSWERS TO MATCHING

1. rejection (p. 279)

2. ego-dystonic (p. 267)

3. ideas of reference (p. 270)

4. Hans Kohut (p. 285)

5. sociopath (p. 271)

6. dialectical behavior therapy (p. 294)

7. circular reasoning (p. 284)

8. abandonment (p. 274)

9. instability of moods (p. 275)

10. Cluster B: dramatic or erratic (p. 267)

11. token economies (p. 294)

12. optimal level of arousal (p. 291)

13. Margaret Mahler (p. 286)

14. problem-solving therapy (p. 288)

15. Ullman and Krasner (p. 287)

16. Hervey Cleckley (pp. 272, 290)

17. symbiosis (p. 286)

18. Cluster A: odd or eccentric (p. 267)

19. females (p. 276)

20. social phobia (p. 280)

21. males (p. 271)

22. splitting (p. 286)

23. Cluster C: anxious or fearful (p. 267)

24. separation-individuation (p. 286)

25. "healthful narcissicsm" (pp. 277, 285)

26. ego-systonic (p. 267)

ANSWERS TO MULTIPLE CHOICE QUESTIONS

1.   c. people whose behaviors appeared to border between neurotic and psychotic. (p. 275)

2.   a. responding to setbacks with depression or fury (p. 272)

3.   c. two in three (p. 283)

4.   c. being temporarily wounded by criticism (pp. 277, 278; p. 286)

5.   b. obsessive-compulsive personality disorder. (pp. 281, 282)

6.   c. histrionic (p. 276)

7.   c. schizotypal personality disorder (p. 270)

8.   c. avoidant personality disorder is to schizoid personality disorder. (pp. 269, 279)

9.   a. behavior therapy and supportive therapy. (p. 294)

10. d. salient childhood experiences. (pp. 285, 287)

11. a. narcissistic (p. 285)

12. a. dependent personality disorder (p. 280)

13. b. preoedipal stage (p. 285)

14. a. ability to learn from experience (p. 273)

15. c. inflated sense of self. (pp. 277, 278)

16. b. borderline personality disorder (p. 275)

17. d. borderline personality disorder (p. 275)

18. a. histrionic personality disorder (p. 276)

19. c. conduct disorder. (p. 271)

20. a. histrionic (p. 276)

21. b. the social and environmental contexts in which the behavior occurs is overlooked. (pp. 282-284)

22. d. all of the above. (p. 293)

23. c. Albert Bandura. (p. 288)

24. c. a personality dimension and a behavioral dimension. (p. 272)

25. c. unfamiliar with the customs and rules of the majority culture. (p. 268)

26. a. people with lower SES levels. (p. 271)

27. a. borderline personality disorder. (p. 274)

28. b. research suggests genetic factors play a role in the development of certain personality disorders (pp. 289-290)

29. d. inhibition (p. 292)

30. b. excessive ambiguity in diagnostic criteria (p. 282)

ANSWERS TO SHORT ANSWER QUESTIONS

1. Personality disorders are characterized by excessively rigid behavior patterns, or ways of relating to others, which ultimately becomes self-defeating. Personality disorders are grouped in the DSM into three clusters. Cluster A personality disorders involve odd or eccentric behavior. Cluster B disorders are characterized by overly dramatic, emotional, or erratic behavior. Cluster C is characterized by anxious or fearful reactions. (p. 267)

2. Cluster A personality disorders are characterized by odd or eccentric behavior, including paranoid personality disorder, schizoid personality disorder, and schizotypal personality disorder. Individuals with paranoid personality disorder are suspicious of the motives of others, but not to the point of delusion. Individuals may be overly sensitive to criticism, whether real or imagined, and take offense at the smallest slight. Schizoid personality disorder is marked by social aloofness and shallow or blunted emotions. Individuals with this disorder lack interest in social relationships and rarely seem to experience strong anger, joy, or sadness. Schizotypal personality disorder is characterized by a persistent difficulty in forming close relationships, in addition to odd or peculiar beliefs or behaviors without clear psychotic features. (pp. 268-270)

3. Cluster B personality disorders are characterized by dramatic, emotional, or erratic behavior, including antisocial personality disorder, borderline personality disorder, histrionic personality disorder, and narcissistic personality disorder. Individuals with antisocial personality disorder display chronic antisocial and irresponsible behavior and lack empathy or remorse for others. An individual must be eighteen years of age for the diagnosis to be applied. An alternative diagnosis of conduct disorder is applied for individuals younger than eighteen years. Borderline personality disorder is marked by tumultuous moods and stormy relationships with others. An individual with borderline personality disorder experiences abrupt shifts in mood, lacks a coherent sense of self, and engages in unpredictable and impulsive behavior. Self-mutilation is sometimes carried out as an expression of anger and means of manipulating others. Histrionic personality disorder is characterized by overly dramatic and emotional behavior, whereby the individual demands to be the center of attention and has excessive need for approval and reassurance. Narcissistic personality disorder is marked by a grandiose sense of self and extreme need for admiration. Individuals with this disorder are often preoccupied with fantasies of success and power, ideal love, or recognition for brilliance and beauty. (pp. 271-278)

4. Cluster C personality disorders are characterized by anxious or fearful behavior, including avoidant personality disorder, dependent personality disorder, and obsessive-compulsive personality disorder. Avoidant personality disorder involves a chronic pattern of avoiding social relationships as the result of fears of rejection. Individuals with avoidant personality disorder are typically unwilling to enter relationships without significant reassurance of acceptance. Individuals with this disorder do have interest in and warmth toward others. However, their fear of rejection prevents involvement in social contact. Dependent personality disorder is characterized by excessive dependence on others and difficulty making independent decisions. Individuals with this disorder have an excessive need to be taken care of. Those with obsessive-compulsive personality disorder have excessive need for orderliness and perfectionism. They pay excessive attention to detail, and relate to others in rigid ways. (pp. 279-282)

5. The reliability and validity of the diagnostic categories pertaining to personality disorders are questionable. Problems resulting in questionable reliability and validity stem from the significant overlap between the diagnoses. Approximately two in three individuals with personality disorders meet diagnostic criteria for more than one type of personality disorder. Certain categories may be based upon sexist assumptions regarding behavior. The agreement between raters on personality disorder diagnoses remains modest at best and the classification system seems to blur the distinction between what is normal and what is not. Finally, there is concern that the diagnoses may confuse labels with explanations leading to circular reasoning. (pp. 282-284)

ANSWERS TO CROSSWORD

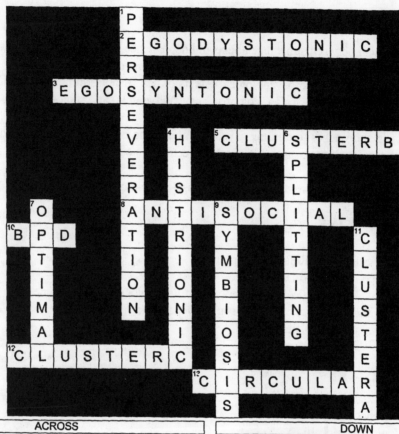

CHAPTER TEN

SUBSTANCE ABUSE AND DEPENDENCE

OBJECTIVES

1. Distinguish between substance abuse and dependence, tolerance and withdrawal.
2. Distinguish between psychological and physiological dependence.
3. Describe physical and psychological effects of depressants, stimulants, and hallucinogens.
4. Discuss biological, learning, cognitive, psychodynamic, and sociocultural perspectives of substance abuse and dependence.
5. Discuss approaches to treating substance abuse and dependence including detoxification, disulfiram, antidepressants, nicotine replacement, methadone maintenance, and naloxone/naltrexone.
6. Discuss the need for and methods of relapse-prevention training.

CHAPTER OUTLINE

Classification of Substance-Related Disorders
        Substance Abuse and Dependence
        Addiction, Physiological Dependence, and Psychological Dependence
        Racial/Ethnic Differences in Substance Dependence
        Pathways to Drug Dependence
Drugs of Abuse
        Depressants
        Stimulants
        Hallucinogens
Theoretical Perspectives
        Biological Perspectives
        Learning Perspectives
        Cognitive Perspectives
        Psychodynamic Perspectives
        Sociocultural Perspectives
Treatment of Substance Abuse and Dependence
        Biological Approaches
        Culturally Sensitive Treatment of Alcoholism
        Nonprofessional Support Groups
        Residential Approaches
        Psychodynamic Approaches
        Behavioral Approaches
        Relapse-Prevention Training
Summing Up

MATCHING

Answers are found at the end of this chapter. Match these terms and concepts with the definitions that follow:

naloxone	amphetamines
withdrawal	heroin
Al-Anon	minor tranquilizers
barbiturates	intoxication
self-control strategies	nicotine chewing gum
freebasing	tolerance
delirium	fetal alcohol syndrome
cirrhosis of the liver	addiction
stimulants	LSD
Korsakoff's syndrome	Antabuse
amphetamine psychosis	endorphins
methadone	detoxification
hashish	relapse prevention training
binge drinking	substance use disorders
withdrawal syndrome	disorientation
analgesia	sedatives
physiological dependence	substance dependence
tachycardia	delirium tremens
psychological dependence	depressant
alcoholism	psychoactive

1. _____ an alcohol-induced disorder that produces confusion, disorientation, and memory loss

2. _____ a slow-acting opiate used in the treatment of heroin addiction

3. _____ neurotransmitters chemically similar to opiate drugs, which are thought to be involved in pleasure and pain experiences

4. _____ a psychoactive substance derived from the resin of a marijuana plant

5. _____ stimulants initially used to extend vigilance, the common abuse pattern is an extended high, followed by a "crash" period of deep sleep and/or depression

6. _____ behavior changes induced by chemical actions of psychoactive substances

7. _____ a pattern of retarded development and features, this affects many children born to mothers who drink during pregnancy

8._____ everyday term for habitual use of a drug accompanied by signs of physiological dependence

9._____ a drug that produces visual hallucinations by decreasing serotonin action and increasing dopamine activity

10._____ a drug that was first developed in 1875 to cure morphine addiction

11._____ disulfiram

12._____ a grouping of therapies that focus on the ABCs of substance abuse

13._____ with continued use of a substance, higher doses are needed to maintain the same effect

14._____ a dramatic reduction in the intake of an abused substance; this produces symptoms characteristic of the specific substance on which the individual is physiologically dependent

15._____ a class of psychoactive substances that increases nervous system activity

16._____ highly addictive depressant drugs used medically to alleviate anxiety and insomnia

17._____ teaching clients how to prevent lapses from resulting in a return to substance dependence

18._____ includes Valium and Librium and are known to produce psychological dependence

19._____ mental confusion and disorientation, combined with inability to focus attention

20._____ the process of heating cocaine powder with ether to release its psychoactive chemical base, which is then inhaled

21._____ a drug-induced state that mimics paranoid schizophrenia

22._____ research supports its use in combination with behavior therapy to stop smoking

23._____ a spin-off of AA, which was designed to provide support for families of alcoholics

24._____ results from a protein deficiency, which is caused by chronic use of alcohol

25._____ a drug that blocks the "high" produced by opiates, effective only in the context of a broader treatment program to help people with substance abuse problems

26._____ the process of helping a physiologically dependent person through withdrawal from the addictive substance

27. _____ having five or more drinks (for men) or four or more drinks (for women) on one occasion

28. _____ a characteristic cluster of symptoms following the sudden reduction or cessation of use of a psychoactive substance after physiological dependence has developed

29. _____ abnormally rapid heartbeat

30. _____ a withdrawal syndrome that occurs following sudden decrease of drinking in individuals with chronic alcoholism

31. _____ compulsive use of a substance to meet a psychological need

32. _____ a drug that lowers the level of central nervous system activity

33. _____ an alcohol-dependence disorder

34. _____ referring to chemical substances that have psychological effects

35. _____ impaired control over the use of a psychoactive substance

36. _____ a condition in which the drug user's body comes to depend on the steady supply of the substance

37. _____ types of depressants that reduce states of tension and restlessness and induce sleep

38. _____ relief from pain without loss of consciousness

39. _____ a state of mental confusion

40. _____ disorders that involve maladaptive use of psychoactive substances

CROSSWORD

Answers are found at the end of this chapter. Complete the following crossword puzzle to reinforce your understanding of this chapter's key terms and concepts:

ACROSS	DOWN
7. habitual use of drug with physiological dependence	1. an alcohol induced syndrome
9. behavior changes induced by psychoactive substances	2. mental confusion
11. spinoff of AA	3. heating cocaine powder and inhaling
13. increase nervous system activity	4. slow acting opiate used for treating heroin addiction
14. psychoactive substance derived from resin of marijuana plant	5. neurotransmitters involved in feelings of pleasure
15. decrease nervous system activity	6. higher doses of drugs needed to produce same effect
	8. symptoms resulting from discontinued use of a drug
	10. affects many children born to mothers who used alcohol in pregnancy
	12. blocks the 'high' produced by opiates

MULTIPLE CHOICE

Answers are found at the end of this chapter. The multiple choice questions listed will test your understanding of the material presented in the chapter. Read through each question and circle the letter representing the best answer.

1. All of the following are true of depressants, except
    a. impairs cognitive processes.
    b. increases central nervous system activity.
    c. in high doses, can arrest vital functions and cause death.
    d. reduces feelings of tension and anxiety.

2. From the use of which two substances may delirium and psychotic disorders be induced during states of intoxication?
    a. alcohol and cocaine
    b. alcohol and nicotine
    c. cocaine and depressants
    d. alcohol and depressants

3. All of the following are examples of substance abuse, except
    a. repeatedly driving while intoxicated.
    b. losing sales due to using cocaine prior to a sales presentation with six major clients.
    c. missing work thirteen days in the last six weeks due to alcohol use.
    d. smoking marijuana at a friend's house on Saturday nights off and on over the past year.

4. The psychedelic drug most likely to induce violent or aggressive behavior is
    a. LSD.
    b. PCP.
    c. THC.
    d. hashish.

5. Which of the following statements is true regarding the use of substances among men and women?
    a. both men and women abuse alcohol and drugs about equally.
    b. the use of depressants such as sedatives and anti-anxiety drugs is higher among men.
    c. men abuse alcohol more while women tend to abuse drugs more.
    d. the rate of tobacco dependence is about equal between men and women.

6. In psychodynamic theory, alcoholism reflects the role of
    a. culture.
    b. oral dependent personality.
    c. anal personality.
    d. negative reinforcement.

7. Which of the following is not a behavioral treatment for substance abuse?
   a. self-control strategies
   b. aversive conditioning
   c. abstinence violation training
   d. social skills training

8. All of the following are diagnostic features of substance dependence, except
   a. tolerance for the substance.
   b. diminished activity in important social, occupational, or recreational activities.
   c. lack of withdrawal symptoms.
   d. continued substance use despite evidence of persistent or recurrent psychological or physical problems associated with its use.

9. Which of the following is true of controlled drinking strategies?
   a. they work best with individuals who can abstain from alcohol.
   b. they help only those with patterns of heavy binge drinking.
   c. they are helpful only for individuals who have gone through withdrawal symptoms during detoxification.
   d. they may be effective with younger drinkers and for those rejecting total abstinence.

10. Which of the following is not part of the common pathway to drug dependence?
   a. experimentation
   b. routine use
   c. regular intoxication
   d. addiction or dependence

11. Which of the following is not a diagnostic criterion for psychoactive substance dependence?
   a. inability to reduce drug use
   b. experiencing intoxication with smaller amounts of the psychoactive substance
   c. spending increased time obtaining, using and recovering from substance use
   d. using the substance to prevent withdrawal symptoms

12. Next to marijuana, this is the most widely used illicit drug in the United States:
   a. heroin.
   b. morphine.
   c. cocaine.
   d. opium.

13. Which of the following is the tendency to overreact to a lapse?
   a. covert sensitization
   b. relapse stigmatization
   c. abstinence violation effect (AVE)
   d. flashback effect

14. Which of the following is true of barbiturates?
    a. quickly produces both physiological and psychological dependence
    b. produces only psychological dependence
    c. produces only physiological dependence
    d. does not produce either physiological or psychological dependence

15. Which of the following is in tobacco smoke?
    a. THC and nicotine
    b. chlorinated hydrocarbons and carbon monoxide
    c. chlorinated hydrocarbons and nicotine
    d. nicotine

16. Through which of the following physiological pathways does alcohol initially produce feelings of relaxation?
    a. heightening the sensitivity of GABA receptor sites
    b. heightening the sensitivity of dopamine receptor sites
    c. decreasing the sensitivity of dopamine receptor sites
    d. decreasing the sensitivity of serotonin receptor sites

17. Modeling explains, in part, why
    a. children of alcoholics drink.
    b. tension reduction occurs with ingestion of alcohol.
    c. genetic factors affect drinking.
    d. self-efficacy is low in drinkers.

18. Risk factors for alcoholism include
    a. sex, age, social class, race, and antisocial personality disorder.
    b. age, social class, alcoholism in the family, mood disorders, and obsessive compulsive personality disorder.
    c. alcoholism in the family, race, depression, and tobacco use.
    d. tobacco use, race, social class, sex, and borderline personality disorder.

19. Which ethnic group more frequently shows a flushing response to alcohol?
    a. Hispanic-Americans
    b. African-Americans
    c. Asian-Americans
    d. Native-Americans

20. Which of the following is the most abused substance in the United States?
    a. alcohol
    b. marijuana
    c. cocaine
    d. caffeine

21. The damaging effects of alcohol abuse appear to be taking the heaviest toll on
    a. Native-Americans; African-Americans
    b. Hispanic-Americans; Native-Americans
    c. Asian-Americans; Irish-Americans
    d. Hispanic-Americans, Asian-Americans

22. High success rates claimed by AA have been criticized on all of the following grounds, except
    a. high percentages are based on personal testimonies rather than careful surveys.
    b. AA is not able to conduct randomized clinical trials in estimating success rate.
    c. the high initial drop out rate is not included in estimating overall success rate.
    d. failure to protect anonymity of clients in analyzing success rates.

23. Fetal alcohol syndrome
    a. requires that the mother drink only during the third trimester of pregnancy.
    b. includes symptoms of narrowly spaced eyes, dwarfism, and mental retardation.
    c. affects all children born to mothers who drink alcohol during pregnancy.
    d. can occur when the mother drinks only one or two ounces of alcohol per day during pregnancy.

24. The research on the efficacy of residential treatment approaches to alcohol abuse support that
    a. residential treatment approaches show the highest rate of success for treating alcohol. abuse when compared with other treatments.
    b. residential treatments are most successful for those people who have a lot of self-control.
    c. most people with alcohol use disorders do not require hospitalization for treatment.
    d. residential treatment approaches have low numbers of early dropouts.

25. Alcoholics Anonymous has adopted many of the ideas and concepts of _____ in its program.
    a. E. Watson
    b. S. Freud
    c. E. Jellinek
    d. S. Freud

26. Repeated high-dosage cocaine use
    a. is nearly always fatal.
    b. can result in anxiety and depression.
    c. raises the threshold of grand-mal seizures.
    d. produces a reverse-tolerance effect.

27. All of the following are opioids, except
    a. morphine
    b. heroin
    c. codeine
    d. PCP

28. Studies investigating the one-drink hypothesis of alcohol suggest that
    a. the biochemical properties of the first alcoholic drink consumed strongly influence the person's decision to continue drinking.
    b. the drinker's expectancies may be more important than the biochemical properties of alcohol in predicting the amount of alcohol consumed.
    c. the biochemical properties of alcohol more strongly influence men's decision to continue drinking than women's decision making to continue drinking.
    d. none of the above.

29. Which of the following has been likened to forms of nonchemical addiction?
    a. depression
    b. alcoholism
    c. pathological gambling
    d. pathological lying

30. Medical problems of cocaine use include all but which of the following?
    a. nasal problems
    b. malnutrition
    c. liver problems
    d. seizures

SHORT ANSWER

Answers are found at the end of this chapter. Answer the following short answer questions:

1.   How do professionals distinguish between drug use and abuse? Between drug abuse and dependence?
2.   What is the difference between psychological and physiological dependence?
3.   What are the risk factors for alcoholism?
4.   What are the pathways to drug dependence?
5.   Discuss the learning perspective as it relates to drug use and abuse.

VIDEO/CD-ROM

In order to obtain greater insight into the information presented in this chapter, refer to the videos that accompany it.

Video 10.1   Substance Abuse: Therapist Jean Obert
Video 10.2   Substance Abuse: Therapist Louise Roberts

ANSWERS TO MATCHING

1. Korsakoff's syndrome (p. 311)

2. methadone (p. 331)

3. endorphins (p. 313)

4. hashish (p. 319)

5. amphetamines (p. 314)

6. intoxication (p. 300)

7. fetal alcohol syndrome (p. 311)

8. addiction (p. 303)

9. LSD (p. 319)

10. heroin (p. 313)

11. Antabuse (p.329)

12. self-control strategies (p. 333)

13. tolerance (p. 301)

14. withdrawal (p. 301)

15. stimulants (p. 314)

16. barbiturates (p. 312)

17. relapse prevention training (p. 334)

18. minor tranquilizers (p. 312)

19. delirium (p. 302)

20. freebasing (p. 315)

21. amphetamine psychosis (p. 314)

22. nicotine chewing gum (p. 330)

23. Al-Anon (p. 332)

24. cirrhosis of the liver (p. 309)

25. naloxone (p. 331)

26. detoxification (p. 329)

27. binge drinking (p. 299)

28. withdrawal syndrome (p. 301)

29. tachycardia (p. 301)

30. delirium tremens (p. 302)

31. psychological dependence (p. 303)

32. depressant (p. 306)

33. alcoholism (p. 306)

34. psychoactive (p. 299)

35. substance dependence (p. 301)

36. physiological dependence (p. 303)

37. sedatives (p. 312)

38. analgesia (p. 313)

39. disorientation (p. 302)

40. substance use disorders (p. 299)

ANSWERS TO MULTIPLE CHOICE QUESTIONS

1. b. increases central nervous system activity. (p. 306)

2. a. alcohol and cocaine (pp. 302, 315)

3. d. smoking marijuana at a friend's house on Saturday nights off and on over the past year. (pp. 300, 301)

4. b. PCP (p. 319)

5. d. the rate of tobacco dependence is about equal between men and women. (p. 317)

6. b. oral dependent personality (p. 327)

7. c. abstinence violation training (pp. 323-325)

8. c. lack of withdrawal symptoms. (p. 301)

9. d. They may be effective with younger drinkers and for those rejecting total abstinence. (p. 336)

10. c. regular intoxication (p. 304)

11. b. experiencing intoxication with smaller amounts of the psychoactive substance (p. 302)

12. c. cocaine (p. 315)

13. c. abstinence violation effect (AVE) (p. 334)

14. a. quickly produces both physiological and psychological dependence (p. 312)

15. d. nicotine (p. 317)

16. a. heightening the sensitivity of GABA receptor sites (p. 310)

17. a. children of alcoholics drink. (p. 325)

18. a. sex, age, social class, race, and antisocial personality disorder (pp. 307, 308)

19. c. Asian-Americans (p. 308)

20. a. alcohol (p. 306)

21. a. Native-Americans; African-Americans (p. 309)

22. d. failure to protect anonymity of clients in analyzing success rates. (p. 332)

23. d. can occur when the mother drinks only one or two ounces of alcohol per day during pregnancy. (pp. 311, 312)

24. c. most people with alcohol use disorders do not require hospitalization for treatment. (p. 333)

25. c. E. Jellinek (p. 310)

26. b. can result in anxiety and depression. (p. 316)

27. d. PCP (pp. 313, 314)

28. b. the drinker's expectancies may be more important than the biochemical properties of alcohol in predicting the amount of alcohol consumed. (pp. 326, 327)

29. c. pathological gambling (pp. 303, 304)

30. c. liver problems (p. 316)

ANSWERS TO SHORT ANSWER QUESTIONS

1. As indicated in the DSM, substance abuse is characterized by a pattern of recurrent use that lead to damaging consequences. The latter may include failure to meet one's responsibilities, problems with the law, putting oneself at physical risk, and social and interpersonal difficulties. The primary feature of substance abuse that distinguishes it from substance use is a pattern of activity which leads to damaging consequences. Substance or drug abuse may progress to substance dependence whereby the individual becomes physiologically dependent upon the drug. (pp. 300, 301)

2. Psychological dependence involves the compulsive use of a substance to meet a psychological need. An individual may rely on a drug to cope with stress without becoming physiologically dependent on the drug. Physiological dependence is a condition whereby the drug user's body comes to depend upon a steady supply of the drug. Major signs of physiological dependence include tolerance and withdrawal syndrome. (p. 303)

3. Risk factors for alcoholism include gender, age, antisocial behavior, family history, and sociodemographic factors. Men are more than twice as likely as women to develop alcohol dependence. This may be the result of both sociocultural and metabolic factors. Alcohol dependence also develops more often in young adulthood, prior to age forty. Antisocial behavior in adolescence and earlier adulthood also increases the risk. The best predictor of alcohol dependence is a family history of dependence. Again, this may be the result of both environmental factors such as modeling and biological factors such a genetic predisposition. Finally, alcohol dependence is more common among low socioeconomic groups than others, as well as those living alone. (pp. 307, 308)

4. There are several pathways to drug dependence. Common pathways to dependence may be describes according to the stages of experimentation, routine use, and finally addiction. During experimentation, use often results in very positive feelings. Individuals during the experimentation stage may feel in control of their behavior and believe they can stop using drugs at any time. During the period of routine use, the individuals may begin to structure their lives around the pursuit and use of the drug. Denial plays a major role. Individuals may deny the extent and consequences of use. As use continues, difficulties in meeting responsibilities and interpersonal problems increase. Dependence may manifest during routine use as users feel powerless to resist the drug. Control is impaired as the individual is physiologically and psychologically dependent on the drug. (p. 304, 305)

5. Learning theorists believe substance abuse is a learned behavior and may be understood within a classical and operant conditioning framework. Drug use may begin and then become habitual because of the reinforcing qualities of the drugs. Drug use may result in positive feelings (positive reinforcement) or provide relief from anxiety and depression (negative reinforcement). As drug use progresses, withdrawal symptoms are alleviated by continued use (negative reinforcement). Classical conditioning principles may account for the cravings experienced by the user. Cravings may be triggered by environmental stimuli associated with use such as the sight of a needle or the smell of an alcoholic beverage. Strong associations between stimuli may lead to frequent cravings, thus perpetuating use. (pp. 323, 324)

ANSWERS TO CROSSWORD

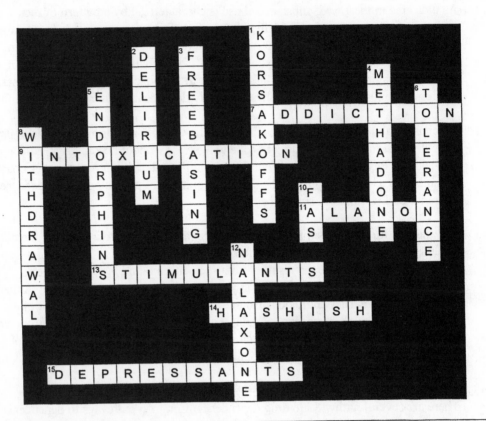

ACROSS	**DOWN**	
7. habitual use of drug with physiological dependence	1. an alcohol induced syndrome	10. affects many children born to mothers who used alcohol in pregnancy
9. behavior changes induced by psychoactive substances	2. mental confusion	12. blocks the 'high' produced by opiates
11. spinoff of AA	3. heating cocaine powder and inhaling	
13. increase nervous system activity	4. slow acting opiate used for treating heroin addiction	
14. psychoactive substance derived from resin of marijuana plant	5. neurotransmitters involved in feelings of pleasure	
15. decrease nervous system activity	6. higher doses of drugs needed to produce same effect	
	8. symptoms resulting from discontinued use of a drug	

CHAPTER ELEVEN

EATING DISORDERS, OBESITY, AND SLEEP DISORDERS

OBJECTIVES

1. Describe the features of anorexia and bulimia and the medical complications associated with each.
2. Explain what causes anorexia and bulimia.
3. Describe the features of binge-eating disorder and how it differs from bulimia.
4. Discuss the treatments of anorexia and bulimia.
5. Discuss the prevalence and causes of obesity.
6. Discuss ethnic and socioeconomic differences in obesity.
7. Discuss the diagnostic features of sleep disorders, the methods of assessing them, and their treatments.

CHAPTER OUTLINE

Eating Disorders
      Anorexia Nervosa
      Bulimia Nervosa
      Causes of Anorexia and Bulimia
      Treatment of Anorexia Nervosa and Bulimia Nervosa
      Binge-Eating Disorder
Obesity: A National Epidemic
      Are You Obese?
      What Causes Obesity?
      Ethnic and Socioeconomic Differences in Obesity
      Facing the Challenge of Obesity
Sleep Disorders
      Dyssomnias
      Parasomnias
      Treatment of Sleep Disorders
Summing Up

MATCHING

Answers are found at the end of this chapter. Match these terms and concepts with the definitions that follow:

bulimia nervosa	binge-eating/purging type
fat cells	obese individuals
dyssomnias	hypnotics
obesity	anorexia nervosa
circadian rhythm sleep disorder	polysomnographic recording
metabolic rate	nightmare disorder
sleepwalking disorder	sleep terrors
restrictive type	systems perspective

compulsive overeaters
binge eating disorder
primary hypersomnia
narcolepsy
amenorrhea
adipose tissue
ABCs of eating
insomnia
hypnagogic hallucinations
antidepressant medication
apnea
sociocultural theories

cataplexy
body mass index
obstructive sleep apnea
parasomnias
REM sleep
exposure with response prevention
osteoporosis
sleep paralysis
rigid dieting
Prozac
eating disorder
hypersomnia

1._____ disorders that are characterized by disturbances in the amount, quality, or timing of sleep

2._____ a disorder characterized by an intense fear of being overweight combined with abnormally low actual weight

3._____ a disorder characterized by recurrent awakenings from sleep because of frightening dreams

4._____ a subtype of anorexia that is characterized by episodes of binge eating and purging, and having a personality that often has problems with impulse control

5._____ the type of medication most commonly prescribed for the use of sleep disorders

6._____ the theory that families regulate themselves in subtle ways to reduce the need for overt change

7._____ cells that actually store fat, they compose the adipose tissue in the body

8._____ a disorder characterized by recurrent cycles of binge eating and purging

9._____ a disorder characterized by episodes in which the sleeper gets out of bed and walks around in the house while remaining fully asleep

10._____ the standard for determining obesity, this takes into account both body height and weight

11._____ binge-eating disorder is more commonly found among these

12._____ a subtype of anorexia that is characterized by severe control over food intake, and having a personality that is obsessively rigid about diet and appearance

13. _____ disorders characterized by abnormal behaviors or physiological events taking place during sleep or at the juncture between sleep and wakefulness

14. _____ sudden loss of muscular control

15. _____ the absence or suppression of menstruation

16. _____ a stage of sleep associated with dreaming

17. _____ measurement of diverse physiological response patterns such as brain waves, eye movements, muscle movements, and respiration

18. _____ terrifying attacks characterized by extreme arousal that happen while asleep

19. _____ a disorder characterized by recurrent eating binges but without subsequent purging

20. _____ a pattern of excessive sleepiness throughout the day for at least one month

21. _____ this is characterized as a chronic medical disease rather than a psychological disorder

22. _____ episodes of partial or complete obstruction of breathing during sleep

23. _____ this disorder is characterized by a disruption in the normal sleep-wake cycle resulting in insomnia or hypersomnia

24. _____ the speed at which food is processed in the body

25. _____ people with BED are often described as these

26. _____ a disorder characterized by sleep attacks during the day

27. _____ fatty tissue in the body

28. _____ behavior modification programs focus on these in the treatment of obesity

29. _____ difficulties falling asleep or remaining asleep

30. _____ occur just before the onset of sleep and tend to involve visual, auditory, tactile, and kinesthetic sensations in those suffering from narcolepsy

31. _____ women with bulimia typically have a history of this

32. _____ class of medication shown to be helpful in the treatment of bulimia

33. _____ a pattern of excessive sleepiness during the day

34. _____ point to societal pressures and expectations placed on young women in our society as contributing to the development of eating disorders

35. _____ a psychological disorder characterized by disturbed patterns of eating and maladaptive ways of controlling body weight

36. _____ temporary cessation of breathing

37. _____ medication that appears to be promising in the treatment of anorexia

38. _____ a temporary state following awakening in which an individual with narcolepsy feels incapable of moving or talking

39. _____ a physical disorder caused by calcium deficiency

40. _____ to eliminate self-induced vomiting, behavioral therapists may use this technique in helping bulimic individuals

CROSSWORD

Answers are found at the end of this chapter. Complete the following crossword puzzle to reinforce your understanding of this chapter's key terms and concepts:

ACROSS			
2.	a subtype of anorexia	15.	disorder involving cycles of binging and purging
4.	involves eating binges without purging		
6.	medications often used for sleep disorders		
7.	cells that compose the adipose tissue in the body		
9.	speed at which food is processed in body		
12.	absence of menstruation		
14.	characterized as chronic medical disease		

DOWN			
1.	standard for determining obesity	13.	characterized by intense fear of being overweight
3.	disorder whereby sleeper gets out of bed and walks around	16.	cessation of breathing during sleep
5.	sudden loss of muscle control		
8.	theory that families regulate themselves		
10.	disorder involving frightening dreams		
11.	disorder involving sleep attacks during day		

MULTIPLE CHOICE

Answers are found at the end of this chapter. The multiple choice questions listed will test your understanding of the material presented in the chapter. Read through each question and circle the letter representing the best answer.

1. In comparison with normal families, families of anorexics and bulimics show more
      a. cohesion.
      b. emotional expression.
      c. conflict.
      d. individuation.

2. Which of the following disorders would be least likely to accompany anorexia or bulimia?
      a. anxiety disorders
      b. dissociative disorders
      c. depression
      d. substance abuse

3. In order to receive a diagnosis of bulimia nervosa, what is the minimum frequency with which a person has to binge or purge?
      a. twice a week for at least three months
      b. four times a week for at least three months
      c. four times a week for at least six months
      d. daily for at least six months

4. The neurotransmitter that may be biologically linked to eating disorders is
      a. dopamine.
      b. serotonin.
      c. GABA.
      d. norepinephrine.

5. Which of the following is not considered to be a dyssomnia?
      a. primary hypersomnia
      b. breathing-related sleep disorder
      c. sleepwalking disorder
      d. circadian rhythm sleep disorder

6. Mary is a twenty nine year old woman who is overweight and often feels depressed. She has tried to lose weight in the past, but her attempts have proven unsuccessful. Although she binges a few times per week when depressed, she has never used laxatives, diuretics, or vomiting to purge herself of the food. Most likely, Mary would be diagnosed with
      a. anorexia nervosa.
      b. bulimia nervosa.
      c. binge eating disorder.
      d. she would not be diagnosed with an eating disorder.

7. Stimulus control techniques used in the treatment of insomnia attempt to
    a. strengthen the connection between bed and sleep by restricting activities done in bed.
    b. strengthen the connection between bed, relaxation, and sleep by encouraging relaxing activities such as watching TV in bed.
    c. strengthen the connection between bed and comforting activities such as eating in order to make the person feel more comfortable in bed.
    d. modify dysfunctional thoughts which interrupt the sleep cycle.

8. One characteristic of young men who may be at higher risk for eating disorders would be
    a. having recently experienced a major illness.
    b. heavy experimentation with drugs.
    c. having a sister with an eating disorder.
    d. being involved in sporting activities that require strict weight maintenance.

9. During which stage of sleep do nightmares generally occur?
    a. stage I
    b. stage II
    c. REM
    d. stage IV

10. The average age of onset for bulimia is
    a. pre-teenage years.
    b. early teenage years.
    c. late teenage years.
    d. late twenties.

11. Research on the sociocultural factors contributing to the onset of eating disorders indicates that
    a. the rates for eating disorders are highest among developing countries.
    b. African American young women have the highest rate of disordered eating behaviors in the United States.
    c. the pressure to achieve an unrealistic standard of thinness has decreased as more Americans have become obese.
    d. four out of five young women in the United States have dieted by their 18th birthday.

12. Which of the following is a feature of sleep-terror disorder?
    a. The experiences are less intense than ordinary nightmares.
    b. Sleep terrors usually last for at least a few hours.
    c. The person does not remember the experience the following morning.
    d. Sleep-terrors disorder typically carries over into adulthood.

13. All of the following are true of insomnia, except
    a. although the sleep disturbance causes fatigue, it does not affect the individual's performance in social, occupational, or other roles.
    b. people with primary insomnia have trouble falling asleep or remaining asleep.
    c. people with primary insomnia have difficulty achieving restorative sleep.
    d. chronic insomnia affects more older people than younger people.

14. Perceiving oneself as fat while others perceive the person as thin is evidence of
    a. an obsession with fat.
    b. a delusion.
    c. distorted body image.
    d. a high body mass index.

15. Regarding obstructive sleep apnea, which of the following statements is false?
    a. The disorder is relatively common.
    b. The disorder is more common in men than in women.
    c. The disorder is more common in individuals who are thin.
    d. Loud snoring may be a sign of obstructive sleep apnea.

16. While cognitive behavioral therapy (CBT) has been demonstrated as one of the most effective treatments for bulimia, about how many patients continue to show evidence of bulimic behavior following treatment?
    a. one-fifth
    b. one-third
    c. one-half
    d. two-thirds

17. Which of the following has the highest rates of obesity?
    a. Black, non-Hispanic women
    b. White, non-Hispanic women
    c. White, non-Hispanic men
    d. Black, non-Hispanic men

18. Which of the following is not a medical complication of anorexia?
    a. neurological problems
    b. dermatological problems
    c. cardiovascular problems
    d. gastrointestinal problems

19. The increase in obesity among Americans is due to
    a. changes in metabolic rates.
    b. lifestyle factors such as high-fat diets and lack of exercise.
    c. genetically determined set points.
    d. predetermined number of fat cells in our bodies.

20. Warren was talking to Brad the other day when he suddenly slumped to the floor fast asleep. He woke up about fifteen minutes later. Warren has been experiencing this phenomenon for a few months now. Which disorder would he most likely have?
    a. primary insomnia
    b. circadian rhythm sleep disorder
    c. narcolepsy
    d. sleepwalking disorder

21. Problems with using drugs to combat insomnia include all but which of the following?
    a. People using these drugs often gain weight.
    b. Sleep-inducing drugs tend to suppress REM sleep.
    c. People using drugs to combat insomnia often experience daytime sleepiness
       and reduced performance.
    d. Rebound insomnia often occurs following discontinuation of the drug.

22. The Greek roots for the term bulimia literally means
    a. without desire for.
    b. sheep graze.
    c. without control.
    d. cow hunger.

23. In a behavioral weight loss program, which of the following would be focused on when teaching
    someone to slow down their pace of eating?
    a. the A's or antecedents of eating
    b. the B's or behaviors of eating
    c. the C's or consequences of eating
    d. the D's or dieting components of eating

24. Psychodynamic theorists emphasize that young women with anorexia
    a. have difficulties with developing separate, individuated identities.
    b. are often the identified patient within a family.
    c. have a weight phobia.
    d. have difficulties reflective of the anal stage of development.

25. Research on effective weight management supports that
    a. regular exercise is crucial for maintaining weight loss.
    b. appetite suppressant medication can be helpful for long-term weight management.
    c. consistent dieting can maintain weight loss.
    d. either consistent dieting or regular exercise alone is sufficient for long-term weight
       management.

26. Research on obesity in children suggests that
    a. one in ten children are overweight.
    b. one in six children are overweight.
    c. one in four children are overweight.
    d. one in three children are overweight.

27. All of the following statements are features of a typical binge, except
    a. the binge usually happens in secret.
    b. a binge does not usually exceed 2,000 calories at a sitting.
    c. the binge is initially pleasant because it signifies a release from dietary restraints.
    d. the binge continues until the binge eater is exhausted, runs out of food, or suffers
       painful stomach distention.

28. Which of the following techniques will encourage adaptive sleep habits?
   a. establishing a regular routine
   b. reading in bed until you feel sleepy
   c. having a daytime nap if you feel sleepy
   d. thinking through tomorrow's schedule while in bed

29. Factors which are associated with increased risk of bulimia include all but which of the following?
   a. childhood sexual and physical abuse
   b. lower self-esteem compared to other dieters
   c. mild concerns about their body weight and shape
   d. engaging in extreme dieting characterized by strict dieting rules

30. Repeated vomiting or abuse of laxatives can cause all but which of the following?
   a. potassium deficiency
   b. tension headaches
   c. bloody diarrhea
   d. decay of tooth enamel

SHORT ANSWER
Answers are found at the end of this chapter. Answer the following short answer questions:

1. List and describe the major types of eating disorders.
2. What are the medical complications associated with anorexia and bulimia?
3. How is binge-eating disorder different than bulimia?
4. List and describe the major types of dyssomnias.
5. List and describe the major types of parasomnias.

VIDEO/CD-ROM
In order to obtain greater insight into the information presented in this chapter, refer to the videos that accompany it.

Video 11.1   Eating Disorders: Nutritionist Alise Thresh
Video 11.2   Anorexia: The Case of Tamora
Video 11.3   Bulimia: The Case of Ann

ANSWERS TO MATCHING

1.dyssomnias (p. 359, 361)

2. anorexia nervosa (p. 341)

3. nightmare disorder (p. 363)

4. binge-eating/purging type (p. 343)

5. hypnotics (p. 365)

6. systems perspective (p. 349)

7. fat cells (p. 355)

8. bulimia nervosa (p. 341)

9. sleepwalking disorder (p. 364)

10. body mass index (pp. 353, 354)

11. obese individuals (p. 351)

12. restrictive type (p. 343)

13. parasomnias (p. 363)

14. cataplexy (p. 362)

15. amenorrhea (p. 343)

16. REM sleep (p. 362)

17. polysomnographic recording (p. 359)

18. sleep terrors (p. 364)

19. binge-eating disorder (p. 351)

20. primary hypersomnia (p. 361)

21. obesity (p. 353)

22. obstructive sleep apnea (p. 362)

23. circadian rhythm sleep disorder (p. 363)

24. metabolic rate (p. 355)

25. compulsive overeaters (p. 351)

26. narcolepsy (p. 362)

27. adipose tissue (p. 355)

28. ABCs of eating (p. 358)

29. insomnia (p. 361)

30. hypnagogic hallucination (p. 362)

31. rigid dieting (p. 347)

32. antidepressant medication (p. 349)

33. hypersomnia (p. 361)

34. sociocultural theories (p. 345)

35. eating disorder (p. 341)

36. apnea (p. 362)

37. Prozac (p. 350)

38. sleep paralysis (p. 362)

39. osteoporosis (p. 343)

40. exposure with response prevention (p. 350)

ANSWERS TO MULTIPLE CHOICE QUESTIONS

1. c. conflict. (p. 348)

2. b. dissociative disorders (p. 341)

3. a. twice a week for at least three months (p. 344)

4. b. serotonin. (p. 349)

5. c. sleepwalking disorder (p. 361)

6. c. binge-eating disorder (p. 351)

7. a. strengthen the connection between bed and sleep by restricting activities done in bed. (p. 366)

8. d. being involved in sporting activities that require strict weight maintenance. (p. 343)

9. c. REM (p. 364)

10. c. late teenage years. (p. 344)

11. d. four out of five young women in the United States have dieted by their eighteenth birthday. (p. 346)

12. c. the person does not remember the experience the following morning. (p. 364)

13. a. although the sleep disturbance causes fatigue, it does not affect the individual's performance in social, occupational, or other roles. (p. 361)

14. c. distorted body image. (p. 343)

15. c. The disorder is more common in individuals who are thin. (p. 362)

16. c. one-half (p. 351)

17. a. Black, non-Hispanic women (p. 357)

18. a. neurological problems (p. 343)

19. b. lifestyle factors such as high-fat diets and lack of exercise. (p. 353)

20. c. narcolepsy (p. 362)

21. a. people using these drugs often gain weight. (p. 365)

22. d. cow hunger. (p. 344)

23. b. the B's or behaviors of eating (p. 358)

24. a. have difficulties with developing separate, individual identities (p. 348)

25. a. regular exercise is crucial for maintaining weight loss. (p. 359)

26. d. one in three children are overweight. (p. 353)

27. b. a binge does not usually exceed 2,000 calories at a sitting. (p. 344)

28. a. establishing a regular routine (p. 367)

29. c. mild concerns about their body weight and shape (pp. 345-348)

30. b. tension headaches (p. 345)

ANSWERS TO SHORT ANSWER QUESTIONS

1. Eating disorders are psychological disorders characterized by disturbed patterns of eating and maladaptive ways of controlling body weight. Included are anorexia nervosa, bulimia nervosa, and binge- eating disorder. Anorexia nervosa involves self-starvation, resulting in a minimal weight for one's age and height or dangerously unhealthy weight. Individuals with anorexia have significant fears of gaining weight and distorted self-image. There are two subtypes of anorexia nervosa: (1) binge-eating/purging type, characterized by episodes of binge eating and purging, and (2) restrictive type, whereby the individual significantly restricts food intake. Bulimia nervosa is characterized by recurrent episodes of binge eating, followed by purging. Unlike individuals with anorexia, individuals with bulimia usually maintain their weight within normal range. Similar to those with anorexia, individuals with bulimia are overconcerned about body weight, and their behavior often leads to medical complications. Both anorexia nervosa and bulimia nervosa typically affect young, Euro-American women. Binge-eating disorder is classified in the DSM as a proposed disorder requiring further study. It is characterized by recurrent eating binges without purging and typically affects obese women who are older than those affected by anorexia or bulimia. (pp. 342-352)

2. Anorexia and bulimia can lead to serious medical complications and can be fatal. The loss of weight seen in anorexia may result in anemia, dermatological problems, cardiovascular complications, gastrointestinal problems, as well as amenorrhea and osteoporosis. The medical complications associated with bulimia often stem from repeat vomiting characteristic of the disorder. Vomiting may result in irritations of the skin, dental problems and abdominal problems. Laxative dependency may cause significant bowel problems. Repeated vomiting and laxative abuse may result in nutritional deficiencies, including potassium deficiency. This, in turn, may lead to cardiac irregularities and even death. (pp. 343, 345)

3. Binge-eating disorder (BED) is characterized by recurrent binge eating without compensatory purging, whereas bulimia nervosa involves episodes of binge eating followed by purging. Furthermore, individuals with BED are often obese women who are older than those affected with bulimia nervosa. Those with bulimia nervosa are typically young women who usually maintain their weight within normal limits. (p. 351)

4. Dyssomnias are sleep disorders involving disturbances in the amount, quality, or timing of sleep, including insomnia, hypersomnia, narcolepsy, breathing-related sleep disorder, and circadian rhythm sleep disorder. Insomnia is characterized by difficulties in falling asleep, remaining asleep, or achieving restorative sleep. Chronic insomnia, which cannot be accounted for by another psychological or physical disorder or by the effects of medication, is referred to as primary insomnia. Hypersomnia is a pattern of excessive sleepiness during the day that continues for a month or longer. Difficulties in daily functioning are common among those with hypersomnia. Narcolepsy is characterized by sleep attacks, accompanied by cataplexy (sudden loss of muscle control) and intrusion of REM sleep. Individuals with narcolepsy also experience sleep paralysis and hypnagogic hallucinations. Breathing-related sleep disorder is characterized by sleep which is repeatedly disrupted by breathing difficulties. The most common type of breathing-related sleep disorder is obstructive sleep apnea, which involves repeated episodes of either complete or partial obstruction of breathing during sleep. Circadian rhythm sleep disorder involves disruption of the internal sleep/wake cycle as the result of time changes in sleep patterns. (pp. 359, 361-363)

5. Parasomnias involve disturbances occurring either during sleep or at the threshold between sleep and wakefulness. Included are nightmare disorder, sleep terror disorder, and sleepwalking disorder. Nightmare disorder is characterized by repeated awakenings as the result of nightmares. The frightening dreams experienced by those with the disorder typically involve lengthy story like dreams that include threats of physical danger. Sleep terror disorder involves recurrent episodes of sleep terror resulting in abrupt awakenings that begin with a panicky scream. Sleep terrors are more intense than nightmares and tend to occur during the first third of nightly sleep and during deep, non-REM sleep. Sleepwalking disorder is characterized by repeated episodes of sleepwalking by an individual who remains asleep. Episodes are of sufficient severity to cause significant personal distress. (pp. 363, 364)

ANSWERS TO CROSSWORD

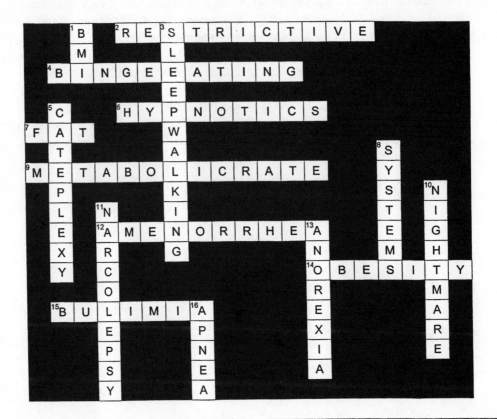

ACROSS		DOWN	
2. a subtype of anorexia	15. disorder involving cycles of binging and purging	1. standard for determining obesity	13. characterized by intense fear of being overweight
4. involves eating binges without purging		3. disorder whereby sleeper gets out of bed and walks around	16. cessation of breathing during sleep
6. medications often used for sleep disorders		5. sudden loss of muscle control	
7. cells that compose the adipose tissue in the body		8. theory that families regulate themselves	
9. speed at which food is processed in body		10. disorder involving frightening dreams	
12. absence of menstruation		11. disorder involving sleep attacks during day	
14. characterized as chronic medical disease			

CHAPTER TWELVE

GENDER IDENTITY DISORDER, PARAPHILIAS,
AND SEXUAL DYSFUNCTIONS

OBJECTIVES

1. Describe sociocultural factors in classifying sexual behaviors as normal or abnormal.
2. Describe the features of gender identity disorder.
3. Describe the process of gender reassignment, and discuss the outcomes of these procedures.
4. Define and describe the features of various paraphilias.
5. Discuss theoretical perspectives on the paraphilias and ways of treating them.
6. Describe the phases of the sexual response cycle.
7. Define and describe the features of various sexual dysfunctions.
8. Discuss theoretical perspectives on sexual dysfunctions and ways of treating them.
9. Discuss the effectiveness of sex therapy techniques.

CHAPTER OUTLINE

Normal and Abnormal in Sexual Behavior
Gender Identity Disorder
 Theoretical Perspectives
Paraphilias
 Exhibitionism
 Fetishism
 Transvestic Fetishism
 Voyeurism
 Frotteurism
 Pedophilia
 Sexual Masochism
 Sexual Sadism
 Other Paraphilias
 Theoretical Perspectives
 Treatment of Paraphilias
Sexual Dysfunctions
 The Sexual Response Cycle
 Types of Sexual Dysfunctions
 Theoretical Perspectives
 Sex Therapy
 Biological Treatments of Male Sexual Dysfunction
Summing Up

MATCHING

Answers are found at the end of this chapter. Match these terms and concepts with the definitions that follow:

fetishism	preorgasmic women
dyspareunia	appetitive phase
voyeurism	gender identity
orgasm phase	sensate focus exercises
transsexualism	frotteurism
sexual dysfunctions	sexual masochism
pedophilia	performance anxiety
sexual impotence	gay bashing
Helen Singer Kaplan	excitement phase
David Barlow	gender identity disorder
exhibitionism	transvestic fetishism
paraphilia	sexual sadism
acquired dysfunction	hypoxyphilia
homosexuality	aversive conditioning
hypoactive sexual desire disorder	vaginismus
male erectile disorder	sexual aversion disorder
heterosexism	resolution phase
female orgasmic disorder	sexual pain disorders
phallic stage	viagra
cognitive behavioral techniques	self-spectatoring

1. _____ sexual dysfunction that begins following a period of normal functioning

2. _____ sexual urges and arousal focused on making a victim suffer humiliation or physical pain

3. _____ women who have never achieved orgasm through any means

4. _____ conflict between biological gender and gender identity

5. _____ the peak and release of sexual tension

6. _____ presence of sexual fantasies and the desire to engage in sexual activity

7. _____ recurrent urges and fantasies regarding sexual activity with prepubescent children

8. _____ sexual arousal to inanimate objects such as clothing

9. _____ persistent feelings of being trapped inside a body with the wrong biological sex

10. _____ Masters & Johnson's therapeutic technique to counter performance anxiety

11. _____ sexual arousal by oxygen deprivation

12. _____ attributed sexual dysfunction to the interaction between immediate and remote causes

13. _____ involves erection in men and vaginal lubrication in women

14. _____ the psychological sense of being male or female

15. _____ violent physical and verbal attacks against lesbians and gay men

16. _____ sexual urges and related fantasies involving cross-dressing

17. _____ fear over ability to perform successfully as a sexual partner

18. _____ pain in the genital region associated with sexual intercourse

19. _____ proposed that anxiety may have inhibiting or arousing effects on sexual response, depending on the male's thought processes

20. _____ sexual urges, arousal and fantasy centered on rubbing against or touching a nonconsenting person

21. _____ persistent or recurrent problems in becoming genitally aroused

22. _____ sexual urges and arousal focused on being humiliated or made to physically suffer

23. _____ involve problems with sexual interest, arousal, or response

24. _____ sexual arousal to stimuli that are unusual or bizarre

25. _____ the recurrent, powerful urge to expose one's genitals to an unsuspecting stranger in order to surprise, shock, or sexually arouse the victim

26. _____ watching unsuspecting people who are undressed, disrobing or engaging in sexual activity in order to attain sexual excitement

27. _____ a sexual orientation characterized by interest in one's own gender

28. _____ a behavioral technique used in the treatment of paraphilias

29. _____ persistent or recurring lack of sexual interest

30. _____ involuntary spasm of the muscles surrounding the vagina resulting in painful intercourse

31. _____ a sexual dysfunction in men characterized by difficulty in achieving or maintaining erection during sexual activity

32. _____ a sexual dysfunction characterized by aversion to and avoidance of genital sexual contact

33. _____ the culturally based belief system that suggests that only reproductive sexuality is psychologically healthy

34. _____ the fourth phase of the sexual response cycle

35. _____ a sexual dysfunction in women involving difficulty reaching orgasm

36. _____ dypareunia and vaginismus are examples

37. _____ psychodynamic theorists focus upon this psychosexual stage when attempting to explain the roots of sexual dysfunctions

38. _____ a medication used to treat erectile problems

39. _____ techniques pioneered by Masters and Johnson

40. _____ the tendency to observe one's behavior as if one were a spectator

CROSSWORD

Answers are found at the end of this chapter. Complete the following crossword puzzle to reinforce your understanding of this chapter's key terms and concepts:

ACROSS		DOWN	
5. feelings of being trapped inside body with wrong biological sex	14. sexual arousal to inanimate objects	1. psychological sense of being female or male	9. phase involving presence of sexual fantasy and desire
8. pain in genital region associated with intercourse		2. focused on making victim suffer physical pain	10. watching unsuspecting people to attain sexual arousal
11. persistent problem becoming genitally aroused		3. rubbing against nonconsenting person	
12. sexual arousal by oxygen deprivation		4. medication used to treat erectile problems	
13. arousal to stimuli that are unusual		6. fourth phase of sexual response cycle	
		7. peak and release of sexual tension	

MULTIPLE CHOICE
Answers are found at the end of this chapter. The multiple choice questions listed will test your understanding of the material presented in the chapter. Read through each question and circle the letter representing the best answer.

1. Sexual behaviors are considered disorders when
    a. they are harmful to others.
    b. they are statistically uncommon in the individual's culture.
    c. the individual experiences personal distress associated with the behavior.
    d. all of the above.

2. Professional stripteasers and swimmers in revealing bathing suits
    a. meet the clinical criteria for exhibitionism.
    b. meet the clinical criteria for transvestic fetishism.
    c. do not meet the clinical criteria for exhibitionism because the individuals they are exposing themselves to are not unsuspecting.
    d. do not meet the clinical criteria for exhibitionism because they are not attempting to sexually arouse the victim.

3. A disorder involving involuntary spasm in the muscles of the vagina which makes sexual intercourse difficult or impossible is
    a. vaginismus.
    b. dyspareunia.
    c. female sexual arousal disorder.
    d. sexual aversion disorder.

4. Recent clinical studies on gender reassignment surgery indicates that
    a. patients tend to have difficulties with social adjustment following the procedure.
    b. patients tend to show favorable outcomes.
    c. patients experience more psychological difficulties than prior to the procedure.
    d. patients typically go through a period of remorse immediately following surgery.

5. Approximately _____ times as many boys as girls have gender identity disorder.
    a. two
    b. three
    c. five
    d. ten

6. An individual who experiences sexual arousal to members of the same sex
    a. are diagnosed ego dystonic homosexual only if they accept their sexual orientation.
    b. are diagnosed bisexual.
    c. are diagnosed ego dystonic homosexual only if they reject their sexual orientation.
    d. none of the above.

7. The view that paraphilias are the result of some object or activity inadvertently becoming associated with sexual arousal, gaining the ability to elicit that arousal when the individual fantasizes about or acts out the paraphilias, is associated with the _____ perspective.
    a. psychodynamic
    b. learning
    c. cognitive
    d. sociocultural

8. Sexual aversion disorder and hypoactive sexual desire disorder are both
    a. sexual desire disorders.
    b. sexual arousal disorders.
    c. orgasm disorders.
    d. sexual pain disorders.

9. Which of the following did the American Psychological Association decide to drop from the DSM in 1973?
    a. premature ejaculation
    b. sexual masochism
    c. homosexuality
    d. transvestic fetishism

10. Research on homophobia suggests all of the following are true of people who are homophobic, except
    a. they tend to have rigid personalities.
    b. they are typically intolerant of anything that deviates from their personal view of appropriate behavior.
    c. they have had previous negative experiences when in direct contact with lesbians or gay men.
    d. none of the above are true.

11. Research suggests that men who are diagnosed with exhibitionism tend to be
    a. angry.
    b. aggressive.
    c. dangerous.
    d. shy.

12. Psychodynamic theorists view gender identity disorder in males as the result of
    a. overly permissive parents.
    b. close mother-son relationships combined with empty father/son relationships.
    c. close father-son relationships combined with empty mother/son relationships.
    d. overly restrictive parents.

13. Freud viewed premature ejaculation as symbolic of
    a. oral fixations.
    b. attachment to the father.
    c. hatred of women.
    d. the electra complex.

14. Psychodynamic theorists view pedophilias as defenses against leftover anxiety from
    a. the anal stage.
    b. the oedipal complex.
    c. the latency stage.
    d. the electra complex.

15. Transvestic fetishism is reported
    a. only among heterosexual men.
    b. only among homosexual men.
    c. only among heterosexual men and women.
    d. only among homosexual men and women.

16. Which of the following is quite commonplace and therefore may not be considered abnormal from the statistical perspective?
    a. frotteurism
    b. paraphilias
    c. sexual dysfunctions
    d. all of the above are considered abnormal from the statistical perspective

17. Behavioral and cognitive therapies for paraphilias attempt to
    a. help the client to accept his or her behavior and fantasies.
    b. help the client adapt his or her behavior to minimize the effect it has on others.
    c. protect society from these individuals.
    d. disconnect arousal from the paraphiliac stimulus and reattach it to normal stimuli.

18. Performance anxiety related to sexual dysfunction is considered to be
    a. a psychological factor.
    b. a biological factor.
    c. a sociocultural factor.
    d. not typically related to sexual dysfunction.

19. All of the following are considered common features of sexual dysfunctions, except
    a. emotional effects.
    b. assumption of a performer role rather than a spectator role.
    c. diminished self-esteem.
    d. fear of failure.

20. _____ is an example of a paraphilia characterized by powerful sexual urges involving receiving humiliation or pain.
    a. Transvestic fetishism
    b. Hypoxyphilia
    c. Sadomasochism
    d. Sexual masochism

21. Which of the following paraphilias is relatively harmless and victimless?
    a. pedophilia
    b. exhibitionism
    c. sadism
    d. fetishism

22. Introduced in 1998, Viagra has helped an estimated _____ percent of patients achieve erections.
    a. 50-60
    b. 60-70
    c. 70-80
    d. 80-90

23. Preorgasmic women are treated most effectively by a program of
    a. directed masturbation.
    b. antidepressant medication.
    c. surgery.
    d. none of the above.

24. Which of the following is an example of transvestic fetishism?
    a. a heterosexual male who cross-dresses in private and imagines himself to be a woman whom he is stroking as he masturbates.
    b. a homosexual male who cross-dresses to attract other men.
    c. a male with a gender identity disorder who cross-dresses because of gender discomfort associated with wearing men's clothing.
    d. all of the above.

25. Which of the following theorists proposed a model of erectile dysfunction that takes into account cognitive factors?
    a. Ellis
    b. Barlow
    c. Kaplan
    d. Johnson

26. Masters and Johnson pioneered the use of _____ which center on enhancing self-efficacy expectancies, improving communication, and fostering sexual competencies.
    a. cognitive behavioral techniques
    b. psychodynamic psychotherapeutic techniques
    c. biological interventions
    d. humanistic behavioral techniques

27. An effective behavioral technique used for the treament of paraphilias is
    a. systematic desensitization.
    b. aversive conditioning.
    c. Viagra.
    d. classical conditioning intervention.

28. Which of the following is not a major paraphilia?
    a. exhibitionism
    b. pedophilia
    c. premature ejaculation
    d. frotterism

29. Sexual gratification associated with acts of rubbing against nonconsenting strangers is known as
    a. sexual sadism.
    b. frotteurism.
    c. pedophilia.
    d. voyeurism.

30. The four phases of the sexual response cycle include
    a. appetitive, excitement, orgasm, and resolution.
    b. appetitive, desire, resolution, and excitement.
    c. excitement, orgasm, avoidance, and communication.
    d. orgasm, resolution, desire, and communication.

SHORT ANSWER
Answers are found at the end of this chapter. Answer the following short answer questions:

1. Where should we draw the line between normal and abnormal sexual behavior? What criteria should we use?
2. How has the classification of homosexuality as a mental disorder changed over the years?
3. List and describe the major types of paraphilias. What are the causes of paraphilias?
4. How do therapists treat paraphilias?
5. What occurs during each of the phases of the sexual response cycle?

VIDEO/CD-ROM
In order to obtain greater insight into the information presented in this chapter, refer to the video that accompanies it.

Video: 12.1   Gender Identity Disorder: The Case of Denise

ANSWERS TO MATCHING

1. acquired dysfunction (p. 385)

2. sexual sadism (p. 382)

3. preorgasmic women (p. 396)

4. gender identity disorder (p. 376)

5. orgasm phase (p. 386)

6. appetitive phase (p. 386)

7. pedophilia (p. 380)

8. fetishism (p. 378)

9. transexualism (p. 372)

10. sensate focus exercises (p. 395)

11. hypoxyphilia (p. 381)

12. Helen Singer Kaplan (p. 394)

13. excitement phase (p. 386)

14. gender identity (p. 372)

15. gay bashing (p. 374)

16. transvestic fetishism (p. 378)

17. performance anxiety (p. 392)

18. dyspareunia (p. 388)

19. David Barlow (p. 390)

20. frotteurism (p. 380)

21. sexual impotence (p. 387)

22. sexual masochism (p. 381)

23. sexual dysfunctions (p. 385)

24. paraphilia (p. 375)

25. exhibitionism (p. 377)

26. voyeurism (p. 379)

27. homosexuality (p. 371)

28. aversive conditioning (p. 383)

29. hypoactive sexual desire disorder (p. 387)

30. vaginismus (p. 388)

31. male erectile disorder (p. 387)

32. sexual aversion disorder (p. 387)

33. heterosexism (p. 375)

34. resolution phase (p. 386)

35. female orgasmic disorder (p. 387)

36. sexual pain disorders (p. 388)

37. phallic stage (p. 389)

38. Viagra (p. 394)

39. cognitive behavioral techniques (p. 394)

40. self-spectatoring (p. 395)

ANSWERS TO MULTIPLE CHOICE QUESTIONS

1. d. all of the above. (p. 372)

2. c. do not meet the clinical criteria for exhibitionism, because the individuals they are exposing themselves to are not unsuspecting (p. 378)

3. a. vaginismus. (p. 388)

4. b. patients tend to show favorable outcomes. (p. 373)

5. c. five (p. 372)

6. c. are diagnosed ego dystonic homosexual only if they reject their sexual orientation. (p. 373)

7. b. learning (p. 382)

8. a. sexual desire disorders. (p. 387)

9. c. homosexuality (p. 371)

10. c. they have had previous negative experiences when in direct contact with lesbians or gay men (p. 374)

11. d. shy (p. 377)

12. b. close mother/son relationships combined with empty father/son relationships. (p. 375)

13. c. hatred of women. (p. 389)

14. b. the oedipal complex. (p. 382)

15. a. only among heterosexual men. (p. 379)

16. c. sexual dysfunctions (p. 385)

17. d. disconnect arousal from the paraphiliac stimulus and reattach it to normal stimuli. (p. 383)

18. a. a psychological factor. (p. 392)

19. b. assumption of a performer role rather than a spectator role. (pp. 392, 393)

20. d. sexual masochism (p. 381)

21. d. fetishism (p. 377)

22. c. 70-80 (p. 394)

23. a. directed masturbation. (p. 396)

24. a. a heterosexual male who cross-dresses in private and imagines himself to be a woman whom he is stroking as he masturbates. (p. 378)

25. b. Barlow (p. 390)

26. a, cognitive behavioral techniques (p. 394)

27. b. aversive conditioning. (p. 383)

28. c. premature ejaculation (p. 384)

29. b. frotteurism. (p. 380)

30. a. appetitive, excitement, orgasm, and resolution (p. 386)

ANSWERS TO SHORT ANSWER QUESTIONS

1. What is considered normal sexual behavior is often dependent upon sociocultural factors. For example, attitudes regarding homosexual behavior range from acceptance to condemnation, dependent upon the culture. Sexual behavior may be considered abnormal if it is self-defeating, is harmful to others, causes subjective distress, impairs one's ability to function, and deviates from social norms. (pp. 371, 372)

2. Homosexuality was once classified as a psychiatric disorder by the American Psychiatric Association. However, the American Psychiatric Association removed homosexuality from its listing of mental disorders in 1973. As noted, attitudes regarding homosexual behavior vary from culture to culture. Although no longer considered a mental illness in the United States, homosexuality is still viewed by some as abnormal. As such, lesbians and gay males continue to be targets of extreme hostility and prejudice. (p. 372)

3. Paraphilias are defined as deviant patterns of sexual gratification, including exhibitionism, voyeurism, sexual masochism, fetishism, frotteurism, sexual sadism, transvestic fetishism, and pedophilia. In each of the paraphilias, sexual graification results from
   a. exposing one's genitals in public (exhibitionism)
   b. observing unsuspecting others who are naked, undressing, or engaging in sexual activity (voyeurism)
   c. receiving humiliation or pain (sexual masochism)
   d. bumping or rubbing against nonconsenting strangers (frotteurism)
   e. inflicting humiliation or pain (sexual sadism)
   f. cross-dressing (transvestic fetishism)
   g. children (pedophilia)

Multiple causes are involved in the development of paraphilias. These may include learning or behavioral factors such as the association of atypical stimuli with sexual arousal. Psychodynamic factors such as unresolved anxiety in childhood, which leads to abnormal patterns of behavior in adulthood, may also be a factor in the development of paraphilias. Sexual or physical abuse may also figure prominently in the etiology of abnormal patterns of sexual gratification. (p. 384)

4. Therapists use a variety of techniques in the treatment of paraphilias, including behavioral interventions such as aversive conditioning and covert sensitization. However, adaptive behavior patterns must also be taught to those with paraphilias. In adition, psychopharmacological interventions such as the use of the antidepressant drug Prozac have shown positive results. (p. 383)

5. The sexual response cycle, as described in the DSM, consists of four distinct phases: appetitive, excitement, orgasm, and resolution phases. The appetitive phase involves sexual fantasy and desire to engage in sexual activity. The excitement phase involves physical changes and feelings of pleasure that occur during the process of sexual arousal. It is during this phase that erection (men) and lubrication (women) occur. The orgasm phase is characterized by the release of involuntary rhythmic contractions of the pelvic muscles, with accompanying feelings of pleasure. The resolution phase entails the sense of well being and relaxation. For a period of time during this phase, men are not able to achieve an erection or orgasm; women, however, are able to maintain high levels of excitement and experience multiple orgasms in succession. (p. 386)

ANSWERS TO CROSSWORD

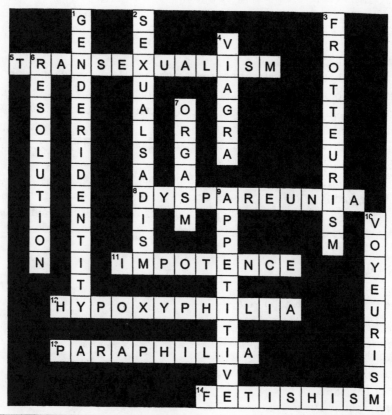

ACROSS		DOWN	
5. feelings of being trapped inside body with wrong biological sex	14. sexual arousal to inanimate objects	1. psychological sense of being female or male	9. phase involving presence of sexual fantasy and desire
8. pain in genital region associated with intercourse		2. focused on making victim suffer physical pain	10. watching unsuspecting people to attain sexual arousal
11. persistent problem becoming genitally aroused		3. rubbing against nonconsenting person	
12. sexual arousal by oxygen deprivation		4. medication used to treat erectile problems	
13. arousal to stimuli that are unusual		6. fourth phase of sexual response cycle	
		7. peak and release of sexual tension	

CHAPTER THIRTEEN

SCHIZOPHRENIA AND OTHER PSYCHOTIC DISORDERS

OBJECTIVES

1. Discuss the historical contributions of Emil Kraepelin, Eugen Bleuler, and Kurt Schneider to the concept of schizophrenia.
2. Describe the diagnostic features of brief psychotic disorder, schizophreniform disorder, delusional disorder, and other schizophrenic spectrum disorders.
3. Review the disturbances in thought, speech, attention, perception, emotions, and other types of impairment associated with schizophrenia.
4. Distinguish between the disorganized, catatonic, paranoid, Type I, and Type II types of schizophrenia.
5. Discuss theoretical perspectives on schizophrenia, including the psychodynamic, learning, biological, and family theories in the development of schizophrenia.
6. Discuss biological, psychodynamic, learning-based, psychosocial-rehabilitation, and family intervention treatments of schizophrenia.

CHAPTER OUTLINE

History of the Concept of Schizophrenia
        Emil Kraeplin
        Eugen Bleuler
        Kurt Schneider
        Contemporary Diagnostic Practices
Other Forms of Psychosis
        Brief Psychotic Disorder
        Schizophreniform Disorder
        Delusional Disorder
        Schizophrenia-Spectrum Disorders
Schizophrenia
        Prevalence of Schizophrenia
        Major Features of Schizophrenia
        Subtypes of Schizophrenia
        Theoretical Perspectives on Schizophrenia
        Treatment Approaches
Summing Up

MATCHING

Answers are found at the end of this chapter. Match these terms and concepts with the definitions that follow:

blocking	second-rank symptoms
persecutory type	Eugen Bleuler
grandiose type	neuroleptics
erotomania	jealous type
ambivalence	mixed type
prefrontal cortex	schizophreniform disorder
tardive dyskinesia	prodromal phase
first-rank symptoms	WHO
brief psychotic disorder	late adolescence
Emil Kraeplin	double-bind communication
residual phase	primary narcissism
neologisms	event-related potentials
waxy flexibility	cross-fostering study
schizophrenia	affect
catatonic type	disorganized type
associations	four As
delusional disorder	erotomanic type
schizoaffective disorder	dementia praecox
perseveration	autism
somatic type	stupor

1._____ a psychotic episode, usually in response to a traumatic event, lasting from one day to one month

2._____ schizophrenic symptoms that have lasted less than six months

3._____ major tranquilizers that can be helpful in alleviating psychotic symptoms

4._____ introduced the term dementia praecox to describe a medical syndrome characterized by mental and behavioral deterioration

5._____ a movement disorder created by long-term use of antipsychotic drugs

6._____ the adoption of a fixed posture, sometimes for very long periods of time

7._____ theorist who characterized schizophrenia as a disorder of the "four A's"

8._____ loving and hating others at the same time

9._____ involuntary interruptions of speech

10._____ evidence points to abnormalities in this area in those with schizophrenia

11._____ according to Kurt Schneider, symptoms that schizophrenia shared with other disorders

12._____ type of delusional disorder involving inflated beliefs about worth

13._____ type of delusional disorder involving delusions of jealousy

14._____ the early period of deterioration in schizophrenia that is characterized by a lessening of interest in social activities and an increase in problems in daily living

15._____ return to the previous level of functioning following the acute episode

16._____ a type of genetic study comparing children whose biological parents either did or did not have a particular disorder and were reared by adoptive parents who either did or did not have that same disorder

17._____ a delusional disorder in which the person believes that he or she is loved by someone else, usually someone famous or representing higher social status

18._____ created words that have no apparent meaning

19._____ brain wave patterns that occur in response to external stimuli, abnormalities in these patterns have been found in schizophrenics

20._____ type of delusional disorder involving themes of being conspired against

21._____ two mutually incompatible messages transmitted simultaneously

22._____ organization that has studied the prevalence of schizophrenia

23._____ type of delusional disorder in which no single theme predominates

24._____ according to Kurt Schneider, symptoms central to the diagnosis of and unique to schizophrenia

25._____ schizophrenia typically develops during this time period

26._____ an early stage of development when the infant has not yet learned that the world and itself are two distinct entities

27._____ an enduring psychotic disorder that involves disturbed patterns of behavior, thinking, emotions, and perception

28._____ emotional responsiveness

29. _____ a type of psychosis characterized by persistent delusions

30. _____ delusional beliefs that someone else is in love with you

31. _____ a type of psychotic disorder in which individuals experience mood disturbances and features associated with schizophrenia

32. _____ term given by Kraepelin to the disorder now known as schizophrenia

33. _____ the persistent repetition of the same thought

34. _____ withdrawal into a private fantasy world

35. _____ delusions involving physical defects, disease, or disorder

36. _____ a state of relative or complete unconsciousness

37. _____ the primary characteristics of schizophrenia

38. _____ relationships among thoughts

39. _____ a subtype of schizophrenia characterized by disorganized behavior, bizarre delusions, and vivid hallucinations

40. _____ a subtype of schizophrenia characterized by gross disturbances in motor activity

CROSSWORD

Answers are found at the end of this chapter. Complete the following crossword puzzle to reinforce your understanding of this chapter's key terms and concepts:

ACROSS	DOWN
1. enduring psychotic disorder	2. subtype of schizophrenia involving gross disturbances in motor activity
9. identifiable factors that may predict vulnerability to schizophrenia	3. persistent repetition of the same thought
10. withdrawal into private fantasy world	4. schizophrenia with clearly identified onset
13. introduced the term dementia praecox	5. major tranquilizers helpful in alleviating psychotic symptoms
14. state of relative unconsciousness	6. relationships among thoughts
15. created words with no apparent meaning	7. early phase of deterioration in schizophrenia
	8. system in the brain which plays a key role in regulating emotions
	11. emotional responsiveness
	12. two mutually incompatible messages

MULTIPLE CHOICE

Answers are found at the end of this chapter. The multiple choice questions listed will test your understanding of the material presented in the chapter. Read through each question and circle the letter representing the best answer.

1. Research on expressed emotion, a type of disturbed family communication, is associated with
    a. higher rates of relapse for schizophrenics following release from the hospital.
    b. better premorbid adjustment.
    c. better prognosis.
    d. the presence of negative symptoms.

2. At what age does schizophrenia usually develop?
    a. early childhood
    b. preteen years and early adolescence
    c. late adolescence and early adulthood
    d. middle adulthood

3. Believing that one's thoughts are somehow transmitted externally so that other people can hear them is
    a. delusions of being controlled.
    b. delusions of grandeur.
    c. thought broadcasting.
    d. thought withdrawal.

4. Which of the following features is unique to schizophrenia?
    a. thought disorder
    b. delusions
    c. hallucinations
    d. none of the above features are unique to schizophrenia

5. Which of the following would not be a component of social skills training for schizophrenics?
    a. psychodrama techniques
    b. role-playing exercises
    c. modeling
    d. direct instruction

6. Regarding the more recent drug, clozapine, which of the following statements is true?
    a. It has some adverse side effects which limits its use with schizophrenics.
    b. It appears to alleviate only positive symptoms of schizophrenia.
    c. It does not affect dopamine receptors in the brain.
    d. It does not appear to be an effective medication for schizophrenics.

7. Which of the following is not one of the types of schizophrenia recognized by the DSM?
    a. simple
    b. disorganized
    c. catatonic
    d. paranoid

8. People who display combined features of schizophrenia and mood disorders are diagnosed with
    a. brief reactive psychosis.
    b. bipolar disorder.
    c. schizoaffective disorder.
    d. schizophreniform disorder.

9. Research on brain abnormalities and schizophrenia supports that
    a. schizophrenics do not have brain abnormalities.
    b. many schizophrenics have abnormal occipital lobe activity, resulting in visual
       hallucinations.
    c. many schizophrenics have abnormally low levels of frontal lobe activity.
    d. many schizophrenics have neurological deficits caused by viral infections.

10. For how long before he or she is diagnosed a schizophrenic must a person show features characteristic of schizophrenia?
    a. thirty days
    b. three months
    c. six months
    d. one year

11. Studies on the genetic component of schizophrenia suggest that
    a. multiple genes are responsible.
    b. a single genetic marker has been identified.
    c. a genetic link is unlikely.
    d. none of the above fit the question.

12. Factors which predict better recovery for schizophrenia include all but which of the following?
    a. higher level of premorbid adjustment
    b. earlier age of onset
    c. a more acute onset
    d. intact neurological functioning

13. The dopamine theory posits that schizophrenics have dopamine receptors that are
    a. overreactive.
    b. underreactive.
    c. blocked.
    d. absent.

14. Which of the following features would be least likely to be characteristic of the residual phase of schizophrenia?
    a. deep sense of apathy and indifference
    b. difficulties thinking and speaking clearly
    c. unusual, odd, or eccentric beliefs
    d. flagrant psychotic behaviors

15. Ventricular enlargement in schizophrenics is associated with
    a. greater evidence of negative symptoms.
    b. poorer premorbid histories.
    c. poorer response to antipsychotic drugs.
    d. all of the above.

16. Which of the following statements is true regarding gender differences in schizophrenia?
    a. men have a less severe course of the disorder
    b. women tend to develop the disorder later
    c. men have achieved a higher level of functioning before the onset of the disorder
    d. all of the above are true

17. A limitation of studying high risk children as a model for the development of schizophrenia is that
    a. high-risk children tend to be uncooperative with research.
    b. high-risk children with a schizophrenic parent have lower IQ scores.
    c. it is not clear whether the "markers" that characterize high risk children with a
       schizophrenic parent will generalize to children without a schizophrenic parent.
    d. so many high risk children develop schizophrenia making it difficult to determine
       valid "markers."

18. The most common type of delusional disorder is the _____ type.
    a. somatic
    b. erotomanic
    c. grandiose
    d. persecutory

19. Research on the treatment of schizophrenia supports that
    a. medication is the most effective means of treatment.
    b. combining psychoanalytic approaches with social skills approaches is most effective.
    c. family intervention programs combined with medication is most effective.
    d. a comprehensive treatment model which incorporates many different treatment
       approaches is most effective.

20. Which of the following theorists was heavily influenced by psychodynamic theory?
    a. Kurt Schneider
    b. Eugen Bleuler
    c. Emil Kraeplin
    d. Paul Meehl

21. The Type I/Type II distinction is similar to the _____ distinction.
    a. reactive/process
    b. simple/undifferentiated
    c. positive/negative symptoms
    d. genetic/behavioral

22. Which of the following disorders may have a common genetic link with schizophrenia?
    a. schizoid personality disorder
    b. schizoaffective disorder
    c. brief psychotic disorder
    d. borderline personality disorder

23. All of the following may be high-risk factors for schizophrenia with the exception of
    a. family conflict, marital discord, and lack of parenting skills.
    b. complications during pregnancy and delivery.
    c. older age of mothers.
    d. poor attentional skills in the preteen to early teenage years.

24. Negative symptoms of schizophrenia
    a. reflect a defect in inhibitory mechanisms.
    b. are associated with better outcome.
    c. appear to reflect the more enduring characteristics of schizophrenia.
    d. are less likely to be present between episodes than positive symptoms.

25. Clanging is an example of which type of disturbance?
    a. disturbance in the form of thought
    b. disturbance in the content of thought
    c. disturbance in the level of functioning
    d. deficit in attention

26. Confused behavior, incoherent speech, inappropriate affect, frequent hallucinations and disorganized delusions are features characteristic of which type of schizophrenia?
    a. Type I
    b. disorganized type
    c. process schizophrenia
    d. paranoid type

27. Which of the following would be an example of a disturbance of volition?
    a. experiencing command hallucinations
    b. lacking interest or drive and unable to pursue a goal
    c. displaying flat affect
    d. speaking in a confused and disordered manner

28. Which of the following is one of Schneider's first rank symptoms?
    a. disturbances in mood
    b. inappropriate affect
    c. ambivalence
    d. delusions

29. If one twin of a pair of monozygotic twins develops schizophrenia, what is the likelihood that the other twin will develop schizophrenia?
    a. less than ten percent
    b. forty to fifty percent
    c. seventy to eighty percent
    d. greater than ninety percent

30. Schizophrenics are
    a. more likely to be distracted by irrelevant stimuli than nonschizophrenics.
    b. less likely to be distracted by irrelevant stimuli than nonschizophrenics.
    c. more likely to ignore relevant stimuli than nonschizophrenics.
    d. more likely to perseverate on relevant stimuli than nonschizophrenics.

SHORT ANSWER

Answers are found at the end of this chapter. Answer the following short answer questions:

1. Describe the clinical features of schizophrenia.
2. List and describe the three major types of schizophrenia.
3. Distinguish between Type I and Type II schizophrenia.
4. Discuss the biological basis of schizophrenia.
5. Discuss interventions used in the treatment of schizophrenia.

VIDEO/CD-ROM

In order to obtain greater insight into the information presented in this chapter, refer to the video that accompanies it.

Video: 13.1   Schizophrenia: The Case of Georgina

ANSWERS TO MATCHING

1. brief psychotic disorder (p. 405)

2. schizophreniform disorder (p. 405)

3. neuroleptics (p. 422)

4. Emil Kraeplin (p. 402)

5. tradive dyskinesia (p. 430)

6. waxy flexibility (p. 417)

7. Eugen Bleuler (p. 402)

8. ambivalence (p. 403)

9. blocking (p. 411)

10. prefrontal cortex (p. 424)

11. second-rank symptoms (p. 403)

12. grandiose type (p. 406)

13. jealous type (p. 406)

14. prodromal phase (p. 408)

15. residual phase (p. 408)

16. cross-fostering study (p. 422)

17. erotomania (p. 407)

18. neologisms (p. 411)

19. event-related potentials (p. 412)

20. persecutory type (p. 406)

21. double-bind communication (p. 425)

22. WHO (p. 409)

23. mixed type (p. 406)

24. first-rank symptoms (p. 403)

25. late adolescence (p. 408)

26. primary narcissism (p. 419)

27. schizophrenia (p. 401)

28. affect (p. 403)

29. delusional disorder (p. 405)

30. erotomanic type (p. 406)

31. schizoaffective disorder (p. 407)

32. dementia praecox (p. 402)

33. perseveration (p. 411)

34. autism (p. 403)

35. somatic type (p. 406)

36. stupor (p. 416)

37. four As (p. 403)

38. associations (p. 403)

39. disorganized type (p. 416)

40. catatonic type (p. 417)

ANSWERS TO MULTIPLE CHOICE QUESTIONS

1. a. higher rates of relapse for schizophrenics following release from the hospital. (p. 426)

2. c. late adolescence and early adulthood (p. 408)

3. c. thought broadcasting. (p. 410)

4. d. none of the above features are unique to schizophrenia. (pp. 409-415)

5. a. psychodrama techniques (p. 433)

6. a. It has some adverse side effects, which limits its use with schizophrenics. (p. 431)

7. a. simple (pp. 416, 417)

8. c. schizoaffective disorder. (p. 407)

9. c. many schizophrenics have abnormally low levels of frontal lobe activity. (p. 424)

10. c. six months (p. 408)

11. a. multiple genes are responsible. (p. 422)

12. b. early age on onset (p. 429)

13. a. overreactive (p. 422)

14. d. flagrant psychotic behaviors (p. 408)

15. d. all of the above (pp. 423, 424)

16. b. women tend to develop the disorder later (p. 409)

17. c. it is not clear whether the "markers" that characterize high-risk children with a schizophrenic parent will generalize to children without a schizophrenic parent. (pp. 420, 421)

18. d. persecutory (p. 406)

19. d. a comprehensive treatment model which incorporates many different approaches is most effective (p. 434)

20. b. Eugen Bleuler (p. 402)

21. c. positive/negative symptoms (p. 418)

22. b. schizoaffective disorder (p. 407)

23. c. older age of mothers. (pp. 428-430)

24. c. appear to reflect the more enduring characteristics of schizophrenia. (p. 418)

25. a. disturbance in the form of thought (p. 411)

26. b. disorganized type (p. 416)

27. b. lacking interest or drive and unable to pursue a goal (p. 415)

28. c. ambivalence (p. 403)

29. b. forty to fifty percent (p. 420)

30. a. more likely to be distracted by irrelevant stimuli than nonschizophrenics. (p. 411)

ANSWERS TO SHORT ANSWER QUESTIONS

1. The clinical features of schizophrenia include disturbed thought processes, attentional deficiencies, perceptual disturbances, emotional disturbances, and other impairments such as confusion regarding self-identity, states of stupor, lack of volition, and impaired social ability. (pp. 409-416)

2. The three major types of schizophrenia, as described in the DSM, include disorganized, catatonic, and paranoid. Disorganized Type schizophrenia is characterized by confused and bizarre behavior, incoherent speech, vivid hallucinations, flat affect, and disorganized delusions. Catatonic Type schizophrenia is arked by gross disturbances in motor activity. Paranoid Type schizophrenia is characterized by the preoccupation with one or more delusions or with the presence of frequent auditory hallucinations. (pp. 416, 417)

3. An alternative manner of subtyping schizophrenia is based on distinguishing Type I from Type II schizophrenia. Type I schizophrenia is characterized by more flagrant symptomatology such as hallucinations, delusions, looseness of associations, abrupt onset, and a more favorable response to antipsychotic medications. The symptoms associated with Type I schizophrenia are known as positive symptoms. Negative symptoms characterize Type II schizophrenia. These include loss or reduction of normal functioning, lack of emotional expression, low or absent levels of motivation, loss of pleasure, isolation, and poverty of speech. Type II schizophrenia is marked by gradual onset and poor response to antipsychotic medication. (p. 418)

4. Twin and adoption research suggest a strong biological basis for schizophrenia, although the specific mode of genetic transmission is unknown. Biochemical factors, such as overactivity of dopamine receptors in the brain, are also implicated. Drugs that block dopamine receptors, resulting in the reduction of dopamine activity, have proven effective in controlling schizophrenic behavior. Research has also pointed to viral agents and other brain abnormalities to address the etiology of this disorder. (pp. 420-424)

5. Biomedical, psychosocial, and family interventions are recommended in the treatment of schizophrenia. As indicated in the diathesis-stress model, schizophrenia may be the result of biological factors coupled with environmental stressors. As such, a comprehensive treatment model would be the most effective in addressing symptomatology. Psychopharmacological treatments may include the use of antipsychotics to control psychotic symptoms. Psychosocial interventions may utilize behavioral methods to improve social skills and enhance adjustment. Family intervention programs may be beneficial to improve communication within the family system to reduce levels of conflict and stress. (pp. 430-434)

ANSWERS TO CROSSWORD

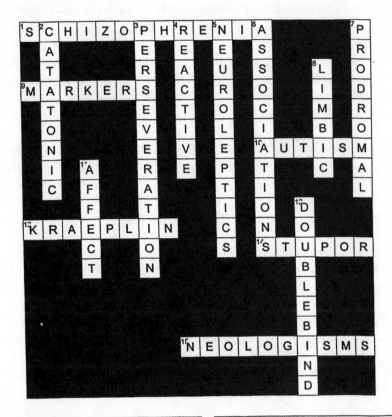

ACROSS	DOWN
1. enduring psychotic disorder	2. subtype of schizophrenia involving gross disturbances in motor activity
9. identifiable factors that may predict vulnerability to schizophrenia	3. persistent repetition of the same thought
10. withdrawal into private fantasy world	4. schizophrenia with clearly identified onset
13. introduced the term dementia praecox	5. major tranquilizers helpful in alleviating psychotic symptoms
14. state of relative unconsciousness	6. relationships among thoughts
15. created words with no apparent meaning	7. early phase of deterioration in schizophrenia
	8. system in the brain which plays a key role in regulating emotions
	11. emotional responsiveness
	12. two mutually incompatible messages

CHAPTER FOURTEEN

ABNORMAL BEHAVIOR IN CHILDHOOD AND ADOLESCENCE

OBJECTIVES

1. Discuss ways of determining what is normal and abnormal in childhood and adolescence.
2. Discuss features, theoretical perspectives, and treatments of autism.
3. Discuss features and causes of mental retardation including, chromosomal, genetic, prenatal, and cultural-familial causes.
4. Discuss types, theoretical perspectives, and interventions for learning disorders.
5. Describe types of communication disorders.
6. Discuss types, features, theoretical perspectives, and treatments of attention-deficit and disruptive behavior disorders.
7. Discuss features and treatment of anxiety disorders and depression in childhood and adolescence.
8. Discuss the problem of adolescent suicide.
9. Discuss theoretical perspectives on enuresis and encopresis and ways of treating them.

CHAPTER OUTLINE

Normal and Abnormal in Childhood and Adolescence
      Cultural Beliefs about What is Normal and Abnormal
      Culturally Sensitive Therapy
      Prevalence of Mental Health Problems in Children and Adolescents
Pervasive Developmental Disorders
      Autism
Mental Retardation
      Causes of Mental Retardation
      Intervention
Learning Disorders
      Types of Learning Disorders
      Theoretical Perspectives
      Intervention
Communication Disorders
Attention-Deficit and Disruptive Behavior Disorders
      Attention-Deficit/Hyperactivity Disorder
      Conduct Disorder
      Oppositional Defiant Disorder
Anxiety and Depression
      Separation Anxiety Disorder
      Perspectives on Anxiety Disorders in Childhood
      Depression in Childhood and Adolescence
Elimination Disorders
      Enuresis
      Encopresis
Summing Up

MATCHING

Answers are found at the end of this chapter. Match these terms and concepts with the definitions that follow:

cuentos	internalized problems
ritalin	savant syndrome
profound mental retardation	cultural-familial retardation
dyslexia	conduct disorder
echolalia	generalized anxiety disorder
aversives	Fragile X syndrome
Leo Kanner	medical model
Turner's syndrome	Tay-Sachs disease
Down syndrome	phenylketonuria
enuresis	play therapy
time-out	encopresis
Klinefelter's syndrome	moderate mental retardation
O. Ivar Lovaas	externalized problems
Asperger's disorder	pervasive developmental disorders
Rett's disorder	childhood disintegrative disorder
autism	mental retardation
cytomegalovirus	learning disorder
psychoeducational model	communication disorder
phonological disorder	ADHD
ODD	hyperactivity

1. _____ a genetic disorder caused by a recessive gene that prevents the child from metabolizing a certain amino acid

2. _____ a high pitched, monotonic repetition of another person's words

3. _____ impoverished social environment producing mental retardation

4. _____ characteristics include a round face, broad flat nose, small hands, and mental retardation

5. _____ includes disorders such as anxiety and depression

6. _____ the most common type of inherited mental retardation

7. _____ a treatment approach in which children enact family conflicts symbolically through their play activities

8. _____ the failure to control one's bowels after the age of four

9. _____ an IQ score of thirty-five to forty-nine would classify an individual in this category

10. _____ found only among females; this is characterized by the presence of a single X chromosome instead of the usual two

11. _____ first to apply the diagnosis of "early infantile autism"

12. _____ a generalized fear or anxiety about past, present, and future events

13. _____ autistic or retarded persons with one exceptional mental ability

14. _____ stories read aloud by therapists or mothers of Puerto Rican children with behavior problems in which the protagonists served as models for adaptive behavior

15. _____ children who purposefully engage in patterns of antisocial behavior that violate social norms and the rights of others may be diagnosed with this

16. _____ an IQ score below 20 would classify an individual in this category

17. _____ a type of punishment, this procedure temporarily removes the child from reinforcing environments

18. _____ characterized by the presence of an extra X sex chromosome; this only occurs in males and results in an XXY sex chromosomal pattern, rather than the XY pattern that men normally have

19. _____ the failure to control one's bladder past the age of five

20. _____ characterizes children who have poorly developed skills in recognizing words and comprehending written text

21. _____ a stimulant drug often used to treat hyperactive children

22. _____ fatal degenerative disease of the central nervous system

23. _____ offered a cognitive learning perspective on treating autism

24. _____ assumes that learning disorders are symptoms of biologically based deficits in cognitive processing

25. _____ includes problems and disorders involving acting out or aggressive behaviors

26. _____ mildly painful stimuli used to control aggressive or destructive behavior

27. _____ a disorder characterized by excessive opposition

28. _____ a pervasive developmental disorder characterized by social deficits without the significant language or cognitive delays associated with autism

29. _____ a pervasive developmental disorder characterized by a loss of previously acquired skills following a period of apparently normal functioning during the first two years of life

30. _____ a pervasive developmental disorder characterized by social deficits, lack of speech, disturbed motor behaviors, and demands for sameness

31. _____ a generalized delay or impairment in the development of intellectual and adaptive abilities

32. _____ a source of infection that carries a risk of mental retardation to the unborn child

33. _____ a class of developmental disorders characterized by significant impaired behavior or functioning in multiple areas of development

34. _____ a pervasive developmental disorder characterized by physical, behavioral, motor, and cognitive abnormalities that begin after a few months of apparently normal development

35. _____ a deficiency in a specific learning ability in the context of normal intelligence

36. _____ an approach used in the treatment of learning disorders which emphasizes children's strengths and preferences rather than correcting underlying deficiencies

37. _____ characterized by difficulties in understanding or using language

38. _____ a type of communication disorders whereby the individual has difficulty articulating the sounds of speech

39. _____ a behavior disorder characterized by excessive motor activity and inability to focus one's attention

40. _____ an abnormal behavior pattern characterized by difficulty in maintaining attention

CROSSWORD

Answers are found at the end of this chapter. Complete the following crossword puzzle to reinforce your understanding of this chapter's key terms and concepts:

ACROSS	
1. failure to control one's bowels	17. characterized by presence of single X chromosome instead of usual two
6. behavior disorder involving excessive motor activity and inability to focus	
8. disorder characterized by excessive opposition	
10. fatal degenerative disease of the CNS	
11. pervasive developmental disorder characterized by social deficits	
13. most common type of inherited mental retardation	
15. temporarily removes child from reinforcing environment	
16. offered a cognitive-learning perspective on autism	

DOWN	
1. high-pitched repetition of another's words	14. a stimulant drug used to treat hyperactive children
2. stories read aloud by therapists or moms of Puerto Rican children	
3. communication disorders with difficulty in articulating sounds	
4. failure to control one's bladder past the age of five	
5. autistic person with exceptional mental ability	
7. syndrome accompanied by mental retardation	
9. poorly developed skills in recognizing words and written text	
12. characterized by demand for sameness	

MULTIPLE CHOICE

Answers are found at the end of this chapter. The multiple choice questions listed will test your understanding of the material presented in the chapter. Read through each question and circle the letter representing the best answer.

1. Which of the following disorders affects approximately three to seven percent of school-age children and is the most common cause of childhood referrals to mental health agencies?
    a. conduct disorder
    b. depression
    c. anxiety
    d. attention-deficit/hyperactivity disorder

2. Disorders of anxiety and depression in childhood are more likely to be found in _____; in adolescence, they are more likely to be found in _____.
    a. boys; boys
    b. girls; girls
    c. boys; girls
    d. girls; boys

3. Although the causes of autism remain a mystery, recent research suggests that _____ plays a significant role in the development of the disorder.
    a. poor parenting
    b. preterm labor
    c. parental divorce
    d. genetics

4. Research indicates that _____ treatment is effective in improving the IQ scores of autistic children.
    a. behavioral
    b. humanistic-existential
    c. drug
    d. psychodynamic

5. For an individual to be diagnosed as mentally retarded, they must meet three of the four diagnostic criteria listed. Which of the following is not one of the criteria for mental retardation?
    a. IQ of seventy or below
    b. history of aggressive behavior
    c. evidence of the disorder before age eighteen
    d. impaired adaptive behavior

6. An infant may be placed on a diet low in the protein phenylalanine to prevent mental retardation due to
    a. Down syndrome.
    b. fetal alcohol syndrome.
    c. PKU syndrome.
    d. cultural-familial retardation.

7. Which of the following is true of amniocentesis?
   a. It is a genetic defect causing blindness.
   b. It is a blood disease of pregnant women.
   c. It a surgical procedure performed seven to twelve weeks following conception.
   d. It involves drawing fluid from the uterus.

8. Treatment based upon which model has produced impressive improvements in the skills of children with learning disabilities?
   a. medical
   b. neuropsychological
   c. psychoeducational
   d. behavioral

9. When a child shows excessive and developmentally inappropriate fear of being removed from his or her mother, which disorder may be experienced by the child?
   a. separation anxiety disorder
   b. conduct disorder
   c. Rhett's disorder
   d. rumination disorder

10. Which of the following is not a symptom of childhood depression?
    a. broad negative expectations for the future
    b. underestimating the consequences of negative events
    c. incorrectly assuming responsibility for negative events
    d. selectively attending to negative aspects of events

11. Which of the following is found only among females?
    a. Fragile X Syndrome
    b. Klinefelters Syndrome
    c. Turner's Syndrome
    d. a and b

12. Which theoretical perspective suggests that functional enuresis is the result of attempting to toilet train too early?
    a. learning/behavioral
    b. genetic
    c. existential
    d. psychodynamic

13. As an adult, a person can perform simple tasks under sheltered conditions, but is incapable of self-maintenance. This person shows _____ mental retardation.
    a. mild
    b. moderate
    c. severe
    d. profound

14. All of the following are examples of externalized problems, except
    a. disruptive behavior.
    b. depression.
    c. aggression.
    d. oppositional behavior.

15. Which of the following is an example of a communication disorder in DSM-IV?
    a. phonological disorder
    b. reading disorder
    c. expressive writing disorder
    d. none of the above

16. Which of the following disorders is considered a pervasive developmental disorder?
    a. Tourette's syndrome
    b. Autism
    c. selective mutism
    d. expressive language disorder

17. This is characterized by an extra or third chromosome on the twenty-first pair of chromosomes, resulting in forty-seven chromosomes, rather than the normal complement of forty-six.
    a. Klinefelter's syndrome
    b. Turner's syndrome
    c. Down syndrome
    d. Tay-Sachs disease

18. All of the following are true of children diagnosed with Attention-Deficit/Hyperactivity Disorder, Combined Type, except that
    a. they tend to do more poorly in school than their peers.
    b. they tend to fidget or squirm in their seats.
    c. they tend to be popular with classmates because they are so outgoing.
    d. they tend to have difficulty following through on instructions.

19. Which of the following factors is not associated with an increased risk of suicide among children and adolescents?
    a. gender
    b. age
    c. race
    d. all of the above are risk factors

20. In 1975, Congress enacted legislation that requires public schools to provide children with disabilities with
    a. educational programs that meet their individual needs.
    b. nutritious, low cost meals.
    c. appropriate tutoring.
    d. all of the above.

21. In Mowrer's bell-and-pad method, the technique is usually explained through principles of
    a. operant conditioning.
    b. classical conditioning.
    c. behavioral modification.
    d. aversive training.

22. The special skills demonstrated by savants are usually associated with which brain functions?
    a. right hemisphere
    b. left hemisphere
    c. hypothalamic
    d. occipital cortex

23. Research on dyslexia points to a possible defect in
    a. a visual relay station.
    b. the thyroid gland.
    c. the substantia nigra.
    d. the autonomic nervous system.

24. All of the following are diagnostic features of autism, except
    a. impaired communication.
    b. impaired inhibitory system.
    c. impaired social interactions.
    d. restricted, repetitive and stereotyped behavior patterns.

25. All of the following are true of Oppositional Defiant Disorder, except
    a. in young children, it is more common among females than males.
    b. it is one of the most common diagnoses among children.
    c. children with this diagnosis tend to be negativistic and defiant of authority.
    d. children with this diagnosis tend to become easily angered or lose their temper.

26. Which of the following is the most common type of learning disorder in children and adolescents?
    a. agraphia
    b. disorder of written language
    c. apraxia
    d. dyslexia

27. The bell-and-pad method is an intervention used to treat _____ in children.
    a. anxiety
    b. depression
    c. enuresis
    d. encopresis

28. Which of the following is considered to be related to Conduct disorder?
    a. attention-deficit hyperactivity disorder
    b. depressive disorder
    c. oppositional defiant disorder
    d. none of the above

29. Autism is caused by
    a. poor parenting
    b. an economically deprived background
    c. poor prenatal care
    d. the causes remain unknown

30. Current research indicates that _____ seems to be the most effective treatment for attention-deficit/hyperactivity disorder.
    a. play therapy
    b. social skills training
    c. stimulant medication
    d. all of the above

SHORT ANSWER
Answers are found at the end of this chapter. Answer the following short answer questions:

1. Discuss the features and etiology of autism.
2. Discuss the prevalence of mental health problems in childhood and adolescence.
3. List and describe attention-deficit and disruptive behavior disorders. What causal factors are related to these disorders?
4. List and describe elimination disorders and childhood. What types of interventions are used for the treatment of these disorders.
5. What are the different types of communication disorders?

VIDEO/CD-ROM
In order to obtain greater insight into the information presented in this chapter, refer to the videos that accompany it.

Video 14.1   Autism: Dr. Kathy Pratt
Video 14.2   ADHD: Dr. Ruth Melmed

ANSWERS TO MATCHING

1. phenylketonuria (p. 450)

2. echolalia (p. 442)

3. cultural-familial retardation (p. 451)

4. Down syndrome (pp. 448, 449)

5. internalized problems (p. 441)

6. Fragile X syndrome (p. 449)

7. play therapy (p. 440)

8. encopresis (p. 473)

9. moderate mental retardation (p. 448)

10. Turner's syndrome (p. 449)

11. Leo Kanner (p. 444)

12. generalized anxiety disorder (p. 466)

13. savant syndrome (p. 453)

14. cuentos (p. 440)

15. conduct disorder (pp. 462-463)

16. profound mental retardation (p. 448)

17. time-out (p. 446)

18. Klinefelter's syndrome (p. 449)

19. eneuresis (p. 472)

20. dyslexia (p. 454)

21. ritalin (p. 461)

22. Tay-Sach disease (p.)

23. O. Ivar Lovaas (p. 445)

24. medical model (p. 456)

25. externalized problems (p. 441)

26. aversive stimuli (p. 446)

27. ODD (p. 463)

28. Asperger's disorder (p. 441)

29. childhood disintegrative disorder (p. 441)

30. autism (p. 443)

31. mental retardation (p. 447)

32. cytomegalovirus (p. 450)

33. pervasive developmental disorders (p. 441)

34. Rett's disorder (p. 441)

35. learning disorder (p. 454)

36. psychoeducational model (p. 456)

37. communication disorder (p. 457)

38. phonological disorder (p. 458)

39. ADHD (p. 459)

40. hyperactivity (p. 459)

ANSWERS TO MULTIPLE CHOICE QUESTIONS

1. d. attention-deficit/hyperactivity disorder (p. 459)

2. c. boys; girls (p. 441)

3. d. genetics (p. 445)

4. a. behavioral (p. 447)

5. b. history of aggressive behavior (p.447)

6. c. PKU syndrome (p. 450)

7. d. It involves drawing fluid from the uterus. (p. 450)

8. d. behavioral (p. 457)

9. a. separation anxiety disorder (p. 466)

10. b. underestimating the consequences of negative events (pp. 468, 469)

11. c. Turner's Syndrome (p. 449)

12. a. learning/behavioral (p. 472)

13. b. moderate (p. 448)

14. b. depression (p. 441)

15. a. phonological disorder (p. 457)

16. b. Autism (p. 441)

17. c. Down syndrome (p. 449)

18. c. they tend to be popular with classmates because they are so outgoing. (pp. 459, 460)

19. d. all of the above are risk factors. (pp. 470, 471)

20. a. educational programs that meet their individual needs. (p. 452)

21. b. classical conditioning. (p. 473)

22. a. right hemisphere (p. 453)

23. a. a visual relay station. (p. 455)

24. b. impaired inhibitory system. (p. 445)

25. a. in young children, it is more common among females than males. (p. 473)

26. d. dyslexia (p. 454)

27. c. enuresis (p. 473)

28. c. oppositional defiant disorder (p. 463)

29. d. the causes remain unknown (p. 445)

30. c. stimulant medication (pp. 461, 462)

ANSWERS TO SHORT ANSWER QUESTIONS

1. Autism is classified as a pervasive developmental disorder. Its major diagnostic features include impairments in social interaction and communication, in addition to restricted, repetitive, and stereotyped behavior patterns. The etiology of autism is not known. However, research has pointed to underlying brain abnormalities possibly resulting from genetic defects or prenatal exposure to toxic agents as possible causal factors. (pp. 443-446)

2. The U.S. Surgeon has reported that one in ten children suffer from a mental disorder severe enough to impair their development. Boys are at greater risk than girls for developing problems such as hyperactivity, autism, elimination disorders, anxiety, and mood disorders. In adolescence, mood disorders and anxiety are more common among girls. Sixty to eighty percent of children with mental health disorders do not receive the treatment they need. This is particularly true regarding internalized problems such as anxiety and depression. (p. 441)

3. Attention-Deficit and Disruptive Behavior Disorders include Attention-Deficit Hyperactivity Disorder (ADHD), Conduct Disorder (CD), and Oppositional Defiant Disorder (ODD). Children with ADHD have problems of impulsivity, inattention, and hyperactivity. Conduct disorder is characterized by antisocial behavior, which violates social norms and the rights of others, whereas ODD includes a pattern of noncompliance and oppositional behavior. Causal factors include family difficulty, including parent/child conflict, marital conflict, and coercive parent/child interactions. In addition, reinforcement for positive behaviors may be lacking. Research has provided information regarding a possible genetic component in the etiology of ADHD. Brain abnormalities may also exist in children with ADHD. (pp. 458-465)

4. Elimination disorders are characterized by persistent problems with controlling urination or defecation that cannot be explained by organic factors. Enuresis is a lack of control over urination, whereas ecopresis is a lack of control over defecation. Behavioral interventions are commonly employed in the treatment of elimination disorders. These include interventions based upon classical conditioning and operant conditioning principles. (pp. 472, 473)

5. Communication disorders are characterized by difficulties in understanding or using language. There are four major types of communication disorders: expressive language disorder, mixed receptive/expressive language disorder, phonological disorder, and stuttering. Expressive language disorder involves impairment in the use of spoken language. A child with this disorder may have difficulties recalling words and producing sentences. Mixed receptive/expressive language disorder is characterized by problems in understanding and producing speech. Phonological disorder involves problems in articulating the sounds of speech in the absence of neurological impairment. Children may omit words or mispronounce certain sounds. Stuttering is characterized by difficulties in fluency. Children who stutter may repeat, prolong and interject inappropriate sounds, substitute words, display an excess of physical tension when speaking, and repeat monosyllabic whole words. (pp. 457, 458)

ANSWERS TO CROSSWORD

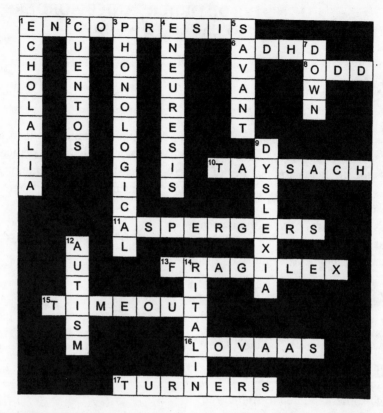

CHAPTER FIFTEEN

COGNITIVE DISORDERS AND DISORDERS
RELATED TO AGING

OBJECTIVES

1. Contrast delirium and dementia.
2. Discuss the features and causes of delirium, dementia, and amnestic disorders.
3. Discuss the basic features of dementia and the relationship between dementia and normal aging.
4. Discuss the problems and features of anxiety, depression, and sleep among older people.
5. Discuss Alzheimer's disease with respect to its incidence, features, progression, biological bases, and treatment.
6. Discuss the features of vascular dementia.
7. Discuss other dementias due to Pick's, Parkinson's, Huntington's, HIV, Creutzfeldt-Jakob disease, head trauma, and neurosyphilis.

CHAPTER OUTLINE

Cognitive Disorders
    Delirium
    Dementia
    Amnestic Disorders
Psychological Disorders Related to Aging
    Anxiety Disorders and Aging
    Depression and Aging
    Sleep Problems and Aging
    Dementia of the Alzheimer's Type
    Vascular Dementia
Dementias Due to General Medical Conditions
    Dementia due to Pick's Disease
    Dementia due to Parkinson's Disease
    Dementia due to Huntington's Disease
    Dementia due to HIV Disease
    Dementia due to Cruetzfeldt-Jakob Disease
    Dementia due to Head Trauma
    Neurosyphillis
Summing Up

MATCHING

Answers are found at the end of this chapter. Match these terms and concepts with the definitions that follow:

delirium tremens
substantia nigra
L-dopa
social withdrawal
Parkinson's disease
GAD
anxiety disorders
insomnia
caudate nucleus
agnosia
dementia
ataxia
Wernicke's disease
tactile
delirium
senile dementias
hypoxia
Korsakoff's syndrome
Alzheimer's disease
plaques

thiamine
aphasia
cerebrovascular accident
stroke
alcohol persisting amnestic disorder
physical decline
multi-infarct dementia
HIV
apraxia
Huntington's disease
general paresis
basal ganglia
physical cause
cognitive disorders
amnestic disorders
presenile dementias
infarction
sleep apnea
neurofibrillary tangles
acetylcholine

1. _____ brain damage due to the blockage of a blood vessel

2. _____ characterized by shaking, tremors, abnormal posture, and lack of control over movements

3. _____ most common type of mental disorder in older adults

4. _____ loss of muscle coordination

5. _____ a form of physical and mental deterioration that results from neurosyphilis

6. _____ associated with depression in later life

7. _____ damage to brain resulting from disruption of blood supply

8. _____ inability to recognize objects despite an intact sensory system

9. _____ loss of ability to speak or understand speech

10. _____ dementia caused by small repeated strokes

11. _____ amnestic disorder results from this

12. _____ group of cell bodies that lie under the cortex and control motor behavior

13. _____ delirium caused by abrupt withdrawal from alcohol

14. _____ dementia is rare in individuals with this

15. _____ characterized by confusion and disorientation, difficulty maintaining balance while walking, and paralysis of the muscles that control eye movements

16. _____ caused by genetic defect on single defective gene

17. _____ difficulty in performing purposeful movements despite an absence of any defect in motor functioning

18. _____ helps control symptoms of Parkinson's disease

19. _____ common among those with Parkinson's disease

20. _____ Huntington's disease involves a progressive deterioration of this in the brain

21. _____ deficiency resulting in Wernicke's disease

22. _____ short and long term memory loss and an inability to form new memories due to chronic alcohol abuse

23. _____ this is actually more prevalent than depression in late adulthood

24. _____ one of the most common anxiety disorders in older adults

25. _____ an abnormal and significant decline in intellectual functioning

26. _____ "black substance" affected in those with Parkinson's disease

27. _____ pertaining to the sense of touch

28. _____ AD patients show reduced levels of this neurotransmitter

29. _____ mental disorders characterized by impaired cognitive abilities and daily functioning

30. _____ a state of extreme mental confusion

31. _____ disturbances of memory associated with an inability to learn new material or recall past events

32. _____ forms of dementia that begin after age 65

33. _____ portions of degenerative brain tissue; associated with AD

34. _____ twisted bundles of nerve cells; associated with AD

35. _____ forms of dementia that begin at or before age 65

36. _____ sudden loss of oxygen to the brain

37. _____ a blockage of the blood vessels supplying the brain

38. _____ a syndrome associated with chronic alcoholism

39. _____ temporary cessation of breathing during sleep

40. _____ a progressive brain disease characterized by gradual loss of memory and intellectual functioning

CROSSWORD

Answers are found at the end of this chapter. Complete the following crossword puzzle to reinforce your understanding of this chapter's key terms and concepts:

ACROSS		DOWN	
4. progressive brain disease characterized by loss of memory	19. temporary cessation of breathing during sleep	1. loss of ability to speak or understand speech	15. vitamin B deficiency producing depression, anxiety, and memory loss
6. inability to recognize objects despite intake sensory system		2. sudden loss of oxygen to the brain	
8. syndrome associated with chronic alcoholism		3. group of cell bodies that control motor behavior	
10. difficulty performing purposeful movements		5. blockage of blood vessels supplying the brain	
13. state of extreme mental confusion		7. characterized by tremors, abnormal posture, shaking	
16. characterized by confusion, disorientation, difficulty with balance		9. result of blockage of a blood vessel	
17. more prevalent than depression in late adulthood		11. portions of degenerative brain tissue	
18. forms of dementias that begin after age 65		12. twisted bundles of nerve cells	
		13. abnormal and significant decline in intellectual functioning	
		14. pertaining to the sense of touch	

MULTIPLE CHOICE

Answers are found at the end of this chapter. The multiple choice questions listed will test your understanding of the material presented in the chapter. Read through each question and circle the letter representing the best answer.

1. The diagnosis of Alzheimer's disease depends upon finding which of the following?
    a. abnormal loss of memory
    b. inability to manage everyday tasks
    c. plaques and neurofibrillary tangles
    d. basal ganglia atrophy

2. Diagnosis of cognitive disorders can be difficult because
    a. damage to the same area of the brain may result in different symptoms for different people.
    b. abnormal behavior patterns found in cognitive disorders resemble those occurring in other mental disorders such as depression.
    c. brain damage may result in a variety of symptoms.
    d. all of the above.

3. Which disorder is a progressive dementia that is similar to Alzheimer's disease and is additionally characterized by social inappropriateness such as the display of flagrant sexual behavior?
    a. Parkinson's disease
    b. Cushing's syndrome
    c. Pick's disease
    d. Huntington's disease

4. Parkinson's disease involves the destruction of brain cells in which area of the brain?
    a. substantia nigra
    b. basal ganglia
    c. cerebral cortex
    d. temporal lobe

5. Which of the following is not a symptom of delirium?
    a. disorientation to time and place
    b. apprehension, fear, or panic
    c. delusions or hallucinations
    d. persistent, irreversible decline in memory

6. Which type of knowledge or memory appears to be fairly resistant to the aging process?
    a. memory associated with timed performance tasks
    b. interpersonal memory
    c. vocabulary and accumulated knowledge
    d. fluid memory

7. Which of the following is not one of the three major types of cognitive disorders?
   a. alcohol-induced disorders
   b. delirium
   c. dementia
   d. amnestic disorders

8. Alzheimer's disease is caused by
   a. overproduction of serotonin.
   b. the body's inability to continue to produce dopamine.
   c. increased levels of acetylcholine (ACh).
   d. unknown causes.

9. Which of the following is a form of dementia that results from repeated strokes?
   a. amnestic thrombosis
   b. vascular dementia
   c. atherosclerosis
   d. all of the above

10. Which of the following statements is false according to the Attitudes Toward Aging Questionnaire?
    a. The occupational performance of the older worker is typically less effective than that of the younger adult.
    b. By age sixty most couples have lost their capacity for satisfying sexual relations.
    c. Most older people are depressed much of the time.
    d. All of the above are false.

11. Which of the following is a possible cause of delirium?
    a. abnormally low levels of thyroxin at birth
    b. an abnormal chromosome
    c. fluid or electrolyte imbalances
    d. the presence of neurofibrillary tangles

12. Which of the following statements regarding HIV infection and dementia is true?
    a. HIV-infected persons with some form of dementia tend to decline faster and die sooner compared to those persons without dementia.
    b. Cognitive impairment typically manifests itself before the AIDS stage of HIV infection.
    c. HIV-infected persons without dementia tend to decline faster and die sooner compared with those persons without dementia.
    d. The first signs of dementia due to HIV disease may mimic the DTs.

13. Several dozen people in Great Britain are believed to have died from eating meat infected with "mad cow disease," which is a variation of which of
    a. Cushing's syndrome.
    b. Cruetzfeldt-Jakob disease.
    c. Huntington's disease.
    d. Pick's disease.

14. Researchers estimate that depressive disorders occur in as many as _____ of stroke victims.
    a. half
    b. one-third
    c. eighty percent
    d. none of the above

15. Which statement is true regarding cognitive disorders?
    a. They involve disturbances in thinking or memory that represent a significant change from the person's prior functioning.
    b. They are caused by medical conditions or drug use or withdrawal from using drugs that affect brain functioning.
    c. They can be short-lived and reversible or chronic and enduring.
    d. All of the above.

16. Which of the following is not a risk factor for depression in older people?
    a. poor health
    b. living alone
    c. lower intelligence level
    d. lower income level

17. Huntington's disease produces all but which of the following symptoms?
    a. jerky movements
    b. unstable mood
    c. violent behavior
    d. memory loss

18. Amnestic disorders are characterized by
    a. the presence of seizures.
    b. profound personality change.
    c. deficits in either short or long-term memory.
    d. gradual decline in intelligence.

19. Which of the following involves a generalized disturbance of the brain's metabolic processes and an imbalance in the levels of neurotransmitters in the brain?
    a. cerebral hemorrhage
    b. dementia
    c. amnesia
    d. delirium

20. Which of the following is not a feature of Alzheimer's disease?
    a. wandering
    b. agitation and aggression
    c. choreiform movements
    d. suspicion, paranoia, and psychotic behavior

21. The offspring of individuals diagnosed with Huntington's disease stand a _____ percent chance of also contracting the disease.
    a. eighty
    b. fifty
    c. ten
    d. one

22. Which of the following is another name for alcohol amnestic syndrome?
    a. Wernicke's disease
    b. beriberi
    c. Korsakoff's syndrome
    d. Pick's disease

23. Research on depression in the elderly supports which of the following?
    a. Caregivers of elderly people suffering from dementia are at risk for depression.
    b. Depression in the elderly is easily recognized by physicians.
    c. People who retire voluntarily are not at risk for depression.
    d. All of the above.

24. An amnestic disorder frequently appears following
    a. a significant life event.
    b. a blow to the head.
    c. a serious physical illness.
    d. ingestion of a drug.

25. Research on the treatment of depression in the elderly suggests that
    a. psychotherapy can be a very effective form of treatment.
    b. drugs are the best treatment for elderly depressed people.
    c. psychotherapy is not appropriate for elderly people.
    d. electro-convulsive shock treatment (ECT) is the most effective form of treatment for depressed elderly people.

26. Depression in later life is associated with
    a. a faster rate of physical decline.
    b. higher mortality rate.
    c. amnestic disorders.
    d. a and b are correct answers.

27. Which of the following statements is not true regarding dementia?
    a. It is typically progressive and irreversible.
    b. The cognitive decline is typically less rapid and severe compared to normal aging.
    c. It most often affects people in later life.
    d. There are more than seventy known causes.

28. Which is the most common type of mental disorders affecting older adults?
    a. mood disorders
    b. anxiety disorders
    c. somatoform disorders
    d. addictions

29. Chronic alcoholism may be a contributing factor in
    a. Graves' disease.
    b. Korsakoff's syndrome.
    c. Addison's disease.
    d. all of the above.

30. When asked, Joe can tell his doctor how to button a shirt, but cannot button his own shirt when asked to do so. Joe may have which of the following deficits?
    a. aphasia
    b. hypoxia
    c. apraxia
    d. agnosia

SHORT ANSWER QUESTIONS

Answers are found at the end of this chapter. Answer the following short answer questions:

1. What are cognitive disorders? List and describe the three major types of cognitive disorders.
2. Describe the features and etiology of Korsakoff's syndrome. Are interventions available for the treatment of Korsakoff's syndrome?
3. Discuss sleep problems associated with aging.
4. Discuss the features and etiology of Alzheimer's disease.
5. Discuss the features and etiology of Parkinson's disease.

VIDEO/CD-ROM

In order to obtain greater insight into the information presented in this chapter, refer to the video that accompanies it.

Video 15.1   Alzheimer's Disease: The Case of Wilburn "John" Johnson

ANSWERS TO MATCHING

1. stroke (p. 493)

2. Parkinson's disease (p. 494)

3. anxiety disorders (p. 485)

4. ataxia (p. 485)

5. general paresis (p. 497)

6. physical decline (p. 486)

7. cerebrovascular accident (p. 493)

8. agnosia (p. 479)

9. aphasia (p. 483)

10. multi-infarct dementia (p. 493)

11. physical cause (p. 483)

12. basal ganglia (p. 495)

13. delerium tremens (p. 482)

14. HIV (p. 496)

15. Wernicke's disease (p. 484)

16. Huntington's disease (p. 496)

17. apraxia (p. 483)

18. L-dopa (p. 495)

19. social withdrawal (p. 495)

20. caudate nucleus (p. 495)

21. thiamine (p. 484)

22. alcohol persisting amnestic disorder (p. 484)

23. insomnia (p. 487)

24. GAD (p. 485)

25. dementia (p. 482)

26. substantia nigra (p. 495)

27. tactile (p. 479)

28. acetylcholine (p. 492)

29. cognitive disorders (p. 480)

30. delirium (p. 481)

31. amnestic disorders (p. 482)

32. senile denentias (p. 482)

33. plaques (p. 489)

34. neurofibrillary tangles (p. 489)

35. presenile dementias (p. 482)

36. hypoxia (p. 484)

37. infarction (p. 484)

38. Korsakoff's syndrome (p. 484)

39. sleep apnea (p. 487)

40. Alzheimer's disease (p. 488)

ANSWERS TO MULTIPLE CHOICE QUESTIONS

1.   c. plaques and neurofibrillary tangles (p. 490)

2.   d. all of the above. (p. 480)

3.   c. Pick's disease (p. 494)

4.   a. substantia nigra (p 495)

5.   d. persistent, irreversible decline in memory (p. 481)

6.   c. vocabulary and accumulated knowledge (p. 485)

7.   a. alcohol-induced disorders (p. 480)

8.   d. unknown causes. (p. 492)

9.   b. vascular dementia (p. 493)

10.   d. All of above are false. (p. 499)

11.   c. fluid or elecrolyte imbalances (p. 482)

12.   a . HIV-infected persons with some form of dementia tend to decline faster and die sooner compared to those persons without dementia. (p. 496)

13.   b. Cruetzfeldt-Jakob disease. (p. 497)

14.   a. half (p. 486)

15.   d. All of the above. (p. 480)

16.   c. lower intelligence level (486)

17.   c. violent behavior (p. 496)

18.   c. deficits in either short- or long-term memory. (pp.482-485)

19.   d. delerium (p. 481)

20.   c. choreiform movements (p. 488)

21.   b. fifty (p. 486)

22.   c. Korsakoff's syndrome (p. 484)

23.   a. Caregivers of elderly people suffering from dementia are at risk for depression. (p. 487)

24.   b. a blow to the head. (p. 483)

25.   a. psychotherapy can be very a effective form of treatment (p. 487)

26.   d. a and b are correct answers. (p. 486)

27.   b. The cognitive decline is typically less rapid and severe compared with normal aging. (p. 482)

28.   b. anxiety disorders (p. 485)

29.   b. Korsakoff's syndrome. (p. 484)

30.   c. apraxia (p. 483)

ANSWERS TO SHORT ANSWER QUESTIONS

1. Cognitive disorders are characterized by disturbances in thinking or memory which represent a significant change from the individual's prior level of functioning. The three major types of cognitive disorders are delirium, dementia, and amnestic disorders. Delirium involves a state of mental confusion, disorientation, and inability to focus one's attention. Dementia is characterized by significant deterioration of mental functioning, including memory. Alzheimer's disease is a type of dementia, involving irreversible and progressive declines in memory and intellectual function. Amnestic disorders involve profound deficits in memory which are not associated with delirium or dementia. An individual with amnestic disorder may be disoriented with regard to time and place. Shot-term or long term memory, or both, may be affected. (pp. 480-484)

2. Korsakoff syndrome, also called alcohol-induced amnestic disorder, is characterized by memory loss and disorientation. Symptoms of Korsakoff's syndrome are caused by thiamine deficiency as the result of poor diet. Thiamine deficiency causes irreversible memory loss. Although significant memory loss may be present, those with Korsakoff's syndrome may retain their general level of intelligence. Treatment interventions to reverse the memory loss seen in those with Korsakoff's syndrome are not available. (pp. 484, 485)

3. Sleep problems are common in late adulthood. These may be the result of physiological changes associated with aging, or may be symptomatic of depression, anxiety, dementia, and medical illness. Psychosocial factors such as isolation and loneliness may also play a role. Sleep apnea, characterized by the cessation of breathing during sleep, may be particularly hazardous as it is linked to an increase risk of dementia and cardiovascular disorder. (p. 487)

4. Alzheimer's disease is a type of dementia characterized by a gradual loss of memory and intellectual functioning, in addition to changes in personality. It is irreversible. Diagnosis of the disorder is typically based on the process of exclusion and when other causes of dementia are ruled out. The early stages of the disease are characterized by limited memory problems and subtle personality changes. As the disease progresses, assistance may be required to manage everyday tasks. Movement and coordination are also affected. In advanced stages of the disease, the individual may experience hallucinations and delusions. The exact cause of Alzheimer's disease is unknown. Multiple causes may be involved. Researchers have investigated the role of genetics in the etiology of the disease. Genetic mutations may play a causal role in the development of plaques seen in the brains of individuals with the disease. Genes which regulate production of certain proteins in the brain, in addition to those in cell metabolism may also have a role. (pp. 488-492)

5. Parkinson's disease is a dementia characterized by muscle tremor, rigidity, difficulty walking, poor control of fine motor movements, lack of facial muscle tone, and cognitive impairment (in certain cases). Parkinson's disease is a progressive disease of the basal ganglia. It is caused by the destruction of dopamine producing cells in the substantia nigra, an area involved in the regulation of movement. The cause of this destruction, however, is unknown. Genetic factors may play a causal role. (pp. 494, 495)

ANSWERS TO CROSSWORD

ACROSS		DOWN	
4. progressive brain disease characterized by loss of memory	19. temporary cessation of breathing during sleep	1. loss of ability to speak or understand speech	15. vitamin B deficiency producing depression, anxiety, and memory loss
6. inability to recognize objects despite intake sensory system		2. sudden loss of oxygen to the brain	
8. syndrome associated with chronic alcoholism		3. group of cell bodies that control motor behavior	
10. difficulty performing purposeful movements		5. blockage of blood vessels supplying the brain	
13. state of extreme mental confusion		7. characterized by tremors, abnormal posture, shaking	
16. characterized by confusion, disorientation, difficulty with balance		9. result of blockage of a blood vessel	
17. more prevalent than depression in late adulthood		11. portions of degenerative brain tissue	
18. forms of dementias that begin after age 65		12. twisted bundles of nerve cells	
		13. abnormal and significant decline in intellectual functioning	
		14. pertaining to the sense of touch	

CHAPTER SIXTEEN

VIOLENCE AND ABUSE

OBJECTIVES

1. Discuss the conditions under which violent behavior may be classified as either normal or abnormal.
2. Discuss the relationship between violent behavior and psychological disorders.
3. Discuss biological, social cognitive, and sociocultural perspectives in explaining human aggression.
4. Discuss the problem of domestic violence, with attention to the psychological characteristics of abusers, patterns of abuse, and sociocultural viewpoints.
5. Discuss the problem of child abuse with respect to the types of abuse, risk factors, effects of abuse, treatment, and prevention.
6. Discuss the incidence of rape, effects, theoretical perspectives, and treatment of rape survivors.
7. Describe the prevalence and patterns of child sexual abuse, the characteristics of abusers, effects on survivors, and efforts directed toward treatment and prevention.
8. Discuss the types, prevalence, and effects of sexual harassment.

CHAPTER OUTLINE

Violence and Abnormal Behavior
       Violence and Psychological Disorders
Explaining Human Aggression
       Biological Perspectives
       Social-Cognitive Perspectives
       Cognitive Perspectives
       Sociocultural Perspectives
       Alcohol and Aggression
       Emotional Factors in Violent Behavior
       Tying it Together
Domestic Violence
       Psychological Characteristics of Male Batterers
       Patterns of Abuse
       Sociocultural Viewpoints
       Effects of Domestic Violence
       Why Don't Battered Women Just Leave?
       Treatment of Batterers and Abused Partners
Child Abuse
       Types of Child Abuse
       Risk Factors in Child Abuse
       Effects of Child Abuse
       Child Abuse Treatment
       Preventing Child Abuse

Sexual Aggression
    Rape
        Child Sexual Abuse
        Sexual Harassment
Summing Up

MATCHING
Answers are found at the end of this chapter. Match these terms and concepts with the definitions that follow:

Albert Bandura
sociobiology
developmental context
Leonore Walker
sexual harassment
anger management training
cognitive theory of aggression
date rape
instinct
physical abuse
empathy training
sexual aggression
death instinct
testosterone
impulse control training
learned helplessness
United States
Alcohol
PTSD
power rape

catharsis
statutory rape
emotional maltreatment
battered woman syndrome
hypothalamus
biological theory of aggression
serotonin
dual diagnosis
disinhibition
limbic system
physical neglect
forcible rape
frustration-aggression hypothesis
social-cognitive perspective
thought conversion
sexual abuse
African Americans
low self-esteem
anger rape
sadistic rape

1. _____ a term that references an individual with a mental illness as well as a chemical addiction

2. _____ according to Freud, an underlying instinct for human aggression

3. _____ a term describing both acts of outright sexual violence as well as sexual harassment

4. _____ an area of the brain that may regulate aggressive behavior

5. _____ training that attempts to increase an offender's sensitivity toward his victim

6. _____ a term used to describe the traumatizing effects of battering

7. _____ constant harsh criticism of a child involving verbally abusive
language or emotional neglect

8. _____ a form of sexual coercion in which a person subjects another person
to unwanted sexual comments, gestures, physical contact, overtures,
or direct demands for sexual favors

9. _____ a theory emphasizing the role of emotional factors in aggressive
behavior

10. _____ the process that involves the loosening of inhibitions or restraints
that normally constrain impulsive behavior

11. _____ a cognitive behavioral treatment approach that helps people identify
and correct anger-inducing thoughts and experiences in various
situations

12. _____ part of the brain involved in regulating primitive drives such as thirst, hunger, and
aggression

13. _____ failure to provide a child with, or withholding from them basic
resources such as food, shelter, and medical care needed to promote
growth and development

14. _____ proposed that aggression is a learned behavior, that is acquired in the same way
as other behaviors

15. _____ coined the term "battered woman syndrome"

16. _____ an inborn pattern of behavior

17. _____ the use of force, violence, or threats to coerce someone into sexual
intercourse

18. _____ the venting of intense emotions or impulses

19. _____ a theory that emphasizes how people interpret confrontative and
conflict situations in explaining aggression

20. _____ an inhibitory neurotransmitter that curbs central nervous system
activity

21. _____ nonaccidental physical injury of a child, ranging from superficial
bruises to death resulting from severe physical injuries

22. _____ the theory that aggressive behavior is an inborn pattern of behavior
that serves a survival function

23. _____ a specific form of acquaintance rape

24. _____ the doctrine which proposes that behavioral traits, like physical
traits, can be transmitted genetically

25. _____ according to psychologist Jay Belsky, this takes into account the intergenerational
transmission of abuse

26. _____ sexual intercourse with someone who is unable to give consent, such
as a child or someone with a mental disability

27. _____ a hormone implicated in aggression

28. _____ proposes that aggression is a learned behavior

29. _____ type of rape that involves torture and bondage

30. _____ type of rape that is motivated by the desire to control the victim

31. _____ type of training whereby students learn problem-solving skills to handle problem
situations

32. _____ process by which victims come to sympathize with their tormentors

33. _____ results from failed attempts to make changes or to obtain results; a psychological factor
which may affect a battered woman's ability to cope

34. _____ the sexual exploitation of children

35. _____ has the highest rate of homicide among young men in developed countries

36. _____ constitute fifty percent of the murder victims in the United States

37. _____ implicated in nearly forty percent of violent crimes

38. _____ a psychological effect of domestic violence

39. _____ more than three-fourths of battered women present evidence of this diagnosable
condition

40. _____ type of rape triggered by feelings of hatred and resentment

CROSSWORD

Answers are found at the end of this chapter. Complete the following crossword puzzle to reinforce your understanding of this chapter's key terms and concepts:

ACROSS	DOWN
1. mental illness combined with chemical addiction	1. acquaintence rape
4. has highest rate of homicide among young men in developed countries	2. process which includes loosening restraints that constrain impulsive behavior
6. coined the term "battered woman syndrome"	3. hormone implicated in aggression
7. may regulate aggressive behavior	5. venting of intense emotions or impulses
11. inborn pattern of behavior	8. type of abuse involving nonaccidental physical injury
12. an inhibitory neurotransmitter	9. implicated in nearly forty percent of violent crimes
15. type of rape triggered by feelings of hatred	10. proposed that aggression is a learned behavior
16. system involved in regulating primitive drives	13. training that attempts to increase sensitivity toward victim
	14. failure to provide basic resources

MULTIPLE CHOICE

Answers are found at the end of this chapter. The multiple choice questions listed will test your understanding of the material presented in the chapter. Read through each question and circle the letter representing the best answer.

1. Which of the following statement is true regarding childhood sexual abuse?
    a. Family members who discover that a child has been abused by a family member are much more likely to report the abuse.
    b. The great majority of cases of sexual abuse involve someone who has some kind of relationship with the child.
    c. Gay males and lesbians account for a disproportionate number of child sexual abusers.
    d. Most fathers who sexually abuse daughters have a satisfying marital relationship.

2. According to your text, we are much more likely to be hurt or killed by _____ than by _____.
    a. someone we know; a stranger
    b. a stranger; someone we know
    c. a police officer; a stranger
    d. a stranger; a police officer

3. A 1997 nation survey showed that 1 in _____ teenagers in the United States carries a weapon.
    a. five
    b. ten
    c. twenty
    d. thirty-five

4. The most common form of child abuse is
    a. physical abuse.
    b. sexual abuse.
    c. emotional maltreatment.
    d. neglect.

5. Which of the following is not considered a factor that may affect a battered woman's ability to cope effectively?
    a. stress-related reactions
    b. lack of financial resources
    c. difficulties handling troubling emotions
    d. learned helplessness

6. An important contributing factor to the high rate of homicides in our country is
    a. the ethnic diversity represented in our country.
    b. the disproportionate number of poor in our country.
    c. easy access to firearms.
    d. all of the above.

7. Research on the effects of media violence suggests which of the following?
    a. TV violence does not contribute to aggressive behavior.
    b. TV violence contributes to aggressive behavior but aggressive children are also more likely to watch it, that is, a circular relationship exists.
    c. aggressive children are less likely to watch TV violence because they are quickly bored by it.
    d. a supportive family does not mitigate the effect of TV violence.

8. Groth and Hobson (1983) hypothesize the existence of three basic types of rape. Which of the following is not included in their hypothesis?
    a. anger rape
    b. power rape
    c. sadistic rape
    d. humiliation rape

9. According to recent statistics, violent crime overall
    a. declined steadily during the early to mid-90s.
    b. increased dramatically in the early 90s and then leveled off.
    c. has remained relatively constant over the past twenty-five years.
    d. dropped dramatically in the late 80s and began a steady incline in the early to mid-90s.

10. That domestic violence is a product of the differential power relationships that exist between men and women in our society is a viewpoint of which theoretical perspective?
    a. cognitive perspective
    b. biological perspective
    c. learning theory perspective
    d. sociocultural perspective

11. Which of the following is a risk factor for childhood sexual abuse?
    a. ethnic background
    b. social class
    c. less cohesive family
    d. children under the age of five

12. Which psychological disorder is associated with a higher risk for violent behavior?
    a. depression
    b. antisocial personality disorder
    c. schizophrenia
    d. narcissistic personality disorder

13. An important risk factor for child abuse is
    a. parental stress.
    b. personality of the child.
    c. lack of previous abuse in the home.
    d. all of the above.

14. Sociocultural research on violence suggests that all but which of the following may contribute to violent behavior?
    a. cultural acceptance of aggressive behavior
    b. gang subculture
    c. higher levels of testosterone in men
    d. social stressors such as unemployment in the home

15. The most widely used form of treatment for sex offenders who are in prison is
    a. most offenders receive little or nothing in the way of psychological treatment in prison.
    b. biologically based treatments such as castration.
    c. individual psychotherapy.
    d. social skills training.

16. Which of the following statements is true regarding rape survivors?
    a. rape survivors only benefit from short term treatment immediately following the rape itself.
    b. most rape survivors receive prompt attention from mental health professionals, crisis teams, and other resources following the rape.
    c. rape survivors with adequate social support do not need additional treatment.
    d. most rape survivors do not seek help from mental health professionals, crisis centers or other resources.

17. The most common type of abuse of girls or boys involves
    a. genital fondling.
    b. sexual intercourse.
    c. punching.
    d. none of the above.

18. According to the frustration aggression hypothesis
    a. the frustration aggression cycle is a learned response that is transgenerational.
    b. frustration leads to aggression, but only under certain circumstances.
    c. frustration and aggression are interrelated; you cannot experience one without the other.
    d. frustration always produces aggression, and aggression is always a consequence of frustration.

19. Which is not an example of sexual harassment?
    a. brushing against a person's body
    b. remarks about a person's body or clothing
    c. forced sexual intercourse
    d. verbal harassment

20. More than half of the rapes committed in this country are against which of the following groups?
    a. females under the age of eighteen
    b. females between the ages of eighteen and thirty
    c. females between the ages of thirty and fifty
    d. females over the age of fifty

21. About one-half of the murder victims in the United States are
    a. non-Hispanic white Americans.
    b. African-Americans.
    c. Asian-Americans.
    d. Hispanic-Americans.

22. Characteristics associated with male batterers include which of the following?
    a. higher income level
    b. lower levels of stress
    c. lack of assertive self-expression
    d. higher educational status

23. PTSD, depression, physical health problems, and sexual dysfunction are possible consequences of which of the following?
    a. emotional neglect
    b. rape
    c. chronic marital relationship dysfunction
    d. sexual harassment

24. Megan's law
    a. ensures that convicted sex offenders are not allowed to hold positions in which they work with children.
    b. requires convicted sex offenders to complete a specific therapeutic program targeting child sexual abuse.
    c. requires convicted sex offenders to register with local police.
    d. all of the above.

25. Alcohol may contribute to aggressive behavior in which of the following ways?
   a. it has a relaxing effect that may make a person less sensitive to cues that serve to inhibit aggressive behavior.
   b. it reduces the capacity to weigh the consequence's of one's behavior, which may lead to aggressive behavior.
   c. it increases the likelihood of misreading the motives of others which may then lead to aggression.
   d. all of the above.

26. According to sociobiologists,
   a. individuals have inherited behavioral traits such as aggression even though such traits may no longer be adaptive.
   b. aggression is the direct result of environmental stresses and demands.
   c. aggression may be modified, but never controlled.
   d. none of the above is true.

27. According to a study by the ECA, individuals who were employed when first interviewed but were later laid off were _____ likely to engage in violent behavior than others who remained employed.
   a. less
   b. six times more
   c. twice as
   d. a third more

28. According to research regarding patterns of abuse,
   a. battering often occurs within a larger pattern of abuse, involving the physical abuse of children and the sexual abuse of spouses.
   b. battering is often an isolated act.
   c. battering is the result of psychogenic conflict.
   d. none of the above is true.

29. All of the following are parental factors associated with an increased risk of child abuse, except
   a. witnessing family violence in one's family of origin.
   b. stress.
   c. being abused during one's own childhood.
   d. all of the above are factors associated with an increased risk of child abuse.

30. Child abuse is associated with an increased risk in later life of
   a. PTSD.
   b. bulimia.
   c. BPD.
   d. all of the above.

SHORT ANSWER

Answers are found at the end of this chapter. Answer the following short answer questions:

1. What criteria are used to classify violent behavior as abnormal?
2. Discuss the neurobiological basis of aggression.
3. Discuss the social-cognitive perspective as it relates to aggression.
4. What are the effects of domestic violence?
5. Why don't all battered women just leave abusive relationships?

VIDEO/CD-ROM

In order to obtain greater insight into the information presented in this chapter, refer to the video that accompanies it.

Video 16.1   Child Sexual Abuse: The Case of Karen

ANSWERS TO MATCHING

1. dual diagnosis (p. 503)

2. death instinct (p. 504)

3. sexual aggression (p. 521)

4. hypothalamus (p. 505)

5. empathy training (p. 511)

6. battered woman syndrome (p. 516)

7. emotional maltreatment (p. 519)

8. sexual harassment (p. 530)

9. frustration aggression hypothesis (p. 510)

10. disinhibition (p. 510)

11. anger management training (pp. 511, 512)

12. limbic system (p. 505)

13. physical neglect (p. 519)

14. Albert Bandura (p. 506)

15. Leonore Walker (p. 516)

16. instinct (p. 504)

17. forcible rape (p. 521)

18. catharsis (p. 504)

19. cognitive theory of aggression (p. 506)

20. serotonin (p. 505)

21. physical abuse (p. 519)

22. biological theory of aggression (pp. 503, 504)

23. date rape (p. 523)

24. sociobiology (p. 504)

25. developmental context (p. 518)

26. statutory rape (p. 521)

27. testosterone (p. 505)

28. social-cognitive perspective (p. 506)

29. sadistic rape (p. 522)

30. power rape (p. 522)

31. impulse control training (p. 511)

32. thought conversion (p. 517)

33. learned helplessness (p. 517)

34. sexual abuse (p. 519)

35. United Sates (p. 501)

36. African-Americans (p. 509)

37. alcohol (p. 509)

38. low self-esteem (p. 515)

39. PTSD (p. 515)

40. anger rape (p. 522)

ANSWERS TO MULTIPLE CHOICE QUESTIONS

1. b. The great majority of cases of sexual abuse involve someone who has some kind of relationship with the child. (p. 518)

2. a. someone we know; a stranger (p. 501)

3. a. five (p. 501)

4. d. neglect (p. 519)

5. b. lack of financial resources (pp. 516-517)

6. c. easy access to firearms. (p. 501)

7. b. TV violence contributes to aggressive behavior, but aggressive children are also more likely to watch it; that is, a circular relationship exists. (p. 507)

8. d. humiliation rape (p. 522)

9. a. declined steadily during the early to mid-90s. (p. 521)

10. d. sociocultural perspective (p. 515)

11. c. less cohesive family (p. 524)

12. b. antisocial personality disorder (p. 503)

13. a. parental stress. (p. 520)

14. c. higher levels of testosterone in men (pp. 508-509)

15. a. most offenders receive little or nothing in the way of psychological treatment in prison. (p. 529)

16. d. most rape survivors do not seek help from mental health professionals, crisis centers or other resources. (p. 524)

17. a. genital fondling. (p. 526)

18. d. frustration always produces aggression, and aggression is always a consequence of frustration (p. 510)

19. c. forced sexual intercourse (p. 530)

20. a. females under the age of eighteen (p. 522)

21. b. African-Americans (p. 509)

22. c. lack of assertive self-expression (p. 514)

23. b. rape (p. 524)

24. c. requires convicted sex offenders to register with local police. (p. 530)

25. d. All of the above. (pp. 509, 510)

26. a. individuals have inherited behavioral traits such as aggression even though such traits may no longer be adaptive. (p. 504)

27. b. six times more (p. 508)

28. a. battering often occurs within a larger pattern of abuse involving the physical abuse of children and the sexual abuse of spouses. (p. 514)

29. d. all of the above are factors associated with an increased risk of child abuse. (p. 519)

30. d. all of the above. (p. 520)

ANSWERS TO SHORT ANSWER QUESTIONS

1. Behavior is considered abnormal if it occurs outside a socially sanctioned context, and is either self-defeating or dangerous to others. (p. 502)

2. Neurobiological research on aggression has focused on structures within the limbic system, in addition to role of neurotransmitters and hormones. The hypothalamus, a structure within the limbic system, may act as a control center for the regulation of aggression. When stimulated in rats and monkeys, violent responses are elicited. The neurotransmitter serotonin may also play a role. Serotonin acts as an inhibitory neurotransmitter within the limbic system, which may regulate violent, impulsive behavior. Studies on adult men who had committed violent crimes indicated low levels of this neurotransmitter. Finally, the male hormone testosterone has been implicated in aggression. High testosterone levels have been correlated to high aggressive dominance in both men and women. (p. 505)

3. Those who adhere to the social-cognitive perspective believe that aggression is a learned response. Modeling and reinforcement play an integral role. Children may learn aggression through exposure to violent models. If children are reinforced for aggression, they are more likely to act aggressively in the future. Expectancies and competencies are also important. Individuals who expect aggressive behavior to produce positive results are more likely to act aggressively. Individuals who lack problem solving abilities may be apt to resolve comflict through aggression. The social-cognitive perspective argues against the psychodynamic notion of catharsis. Social-cognitive theorists do not believe the expression of aggression will reduce the potential for aggression. According to this

perspective, we should expect the potential for aggression to be more likely after its expression. This is especially true if the aggressive act was reinforced. (p. 506)

4. In addition to physical injury, domestic violence leads to a variety of psychological effects, including post-traumatic stress disorder (PTSD), depression, and low self-esteem. More than three fourths of battered women may be diagnosed with PTSD. Domestic violence may also be a contributing factor in substance abuse disorders, as victims attempt to self-medicate. The toll on children is significant. Children who have witnessed violence are at risk for behavioral and emotional problems. Parental modeling of violence may also set the stage for intergenerational violence. (p. 515)

5. Approximately fifty percent of women who seek professional assistance for domestic violence return to their abusive partners. Battered woman syndrome may account for this behavior. Battered woman syndrome is characterized by feelings of helplessness and impaired coping ability. It is the result of the traumatizing effects of abuse. In addition, women may not leave their partners because of economic concerns and fear of homelessness. Several psychological factors have been identified that may affect a woman's ability to cope effectively within an abusive context. These include shattering the myth of personal invulnerability, reduced problem-solving ability, stress related reactions, thought conversion, finding meaning in the abuse, learned helplessness, and difficulty handling troubled emotions. (pp. 516, 517)

ANSWERS TO CROSSWORD

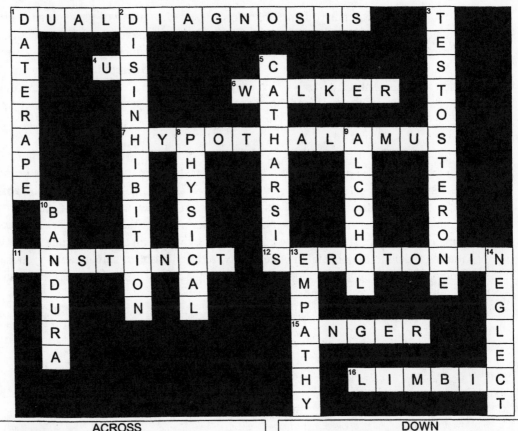

ACROSS	DOWN
1. mental illness combined with chemical addiction	1. acquaintence rape
4. has highest rate of homicide among young men in developed countries	2. process which includes loosening restraints that constrain impulsive behavior
6. coined the term "battered woman syndrome"	3. hormone implicated in aggression
7. may regulate aggressive behavior	5. venting of intense emotions or impulses
11. inborn pattern of behavior	8. type of abuse involving nonaccidental physical injury
12. an inhibitory neurotransmitter	9. implicated in nearly forty percent of violent crimes
15. type of rape triggered by feelings of hatred	10. proposed that aggression is a learned behavior
16. system involved in regulating primitive drives	13. training that attempts to increase sensitivity toward victim
	14. failure to provide basic resources

CHAPTER SEVENTEEN

ABNORMAL PSYCHOLOGY AND SOCIETY

OBJECTIVES

1. Describe the legal procedures for psychiatric commitment and the safeguards to prevent abuses of psychiatric commitment.
2. Discuss the controversy concerning psychiatric commitment.
3. Discuss the problem faced by psychologists and other professionals who are given the task of attempting to predict dangerousness.
4. Discuss the "duty to warn" obligation for therapists and describe the landmark case on which it is based.
5. Discuss the legal basis of the right to treatment and the right to refuse treatment.
6. Discuss landmark cases that establish the legal precedents for the insanity plea.
7. Distinguish between the insanity plea and the principle of competency to stand trial.

CHAPTER OUTLINE

Psychiatric Commitment and Patient's Rights
        Predicting Dangerousness
        Hoc Problem
        Patient's Rights
The Insanity Defense
        Legal Bases of the Insanity Defense
        Determining the Length of Criminal Commitment
        Perspectives on the Insanity Defense
        Competency to Stand Trial
Summing Up

MATCHING

Answers are found at the end of this chapter. Match these terms and concepts with the definitions that follow:

Medina v. California	false negative
ALI guideline	Rogers v. Okin
legal commitment	base-rate problem
O'Connor v. Donaldson	Addington v. Texas
insanity defense	Durham v. United States
Youngberg v. Romeo	Wyatt v. Stickney
Jones v. United States	post hoc problem
civil commitment	duty to warn
false positive	GBMI
M'Naghten rule	Tarasoff v. Regents of the University of California
competent to stand trial	voluntary hospitalization

1. _____ may happen when a person is a threat to him or herself or others

2. _____ insane because one cannot tell right from wrong

3. _____ the relative difficulty of making predictions of rare or infrequent events

4. _____ indeterminate commitment is legal for those not guilty through insanity

5. _____ allows a person to leave a psychiatric institution when he or she want to

6. _____ a person who is capable of understanding criminal charges and proceedings

7. _____ no involuntary commitment for persons who are not dangerous

8. _____ instrumental in encouraging a number of states to shift the burden of proof from the federal prosecutor to the defense to prove insanity

9. _____ may happen when a person commits a crime due to a mental disorder or defect

10. _____ incorrectly failing to predict the occurrence of a behavior when it actually happens

11. _____ the burden of proof for determining incompetence to stand trial lies with the defendant, not the state

12. _____ requires therapists to reveal confidential information to protect third parties

13. _____ combines the M'Naghten principle with the irresistible impulse principle

14. _____ treatment for the confined in reasonable safety

15. _____ the claim of being not guilty due to a mental defect or disorder

16. _____ incorrectly predicting the occurrence of a behavior when it actually does not happen

17. _____ minimum standard of care for psychiatric hospitals

18. _____ psychotropic medications cannot be forced upon involuntarily committed patients

19. _____ in order for individuals to be hospitalized involuntarily, they must be judged both to be 'mentally ill' and to present a clear and present danger to themselves or others

20. _____ recognizing violent tendencies after a violent incident occurs

21. _____ the therapist's obligation to warn third parties of threats made against them by clients

22. _____ offers juries the option of finding a defendant both guilty and mentally ill

CROSSWORD

Answers are found at the end of this chapter. Complete the following crossword puzzle to reinforce your understanding of this chapter's key terms and concepts:

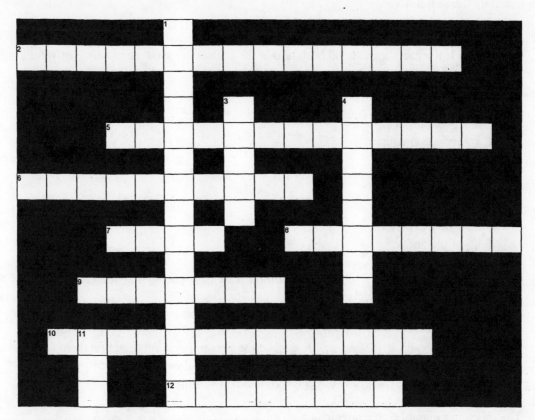

ACROSS	DOWN
2. claiming one is not guilty because of a mental defect	1. may occur if person is a threat to others
5. incorrectly failing to predict behavior when it actually happens	3. type of commitment that may occur if the person commits a crime
6. obligation to warn third parties of threats	4. problem involving difficulty predicting dangerousness from rare cases
7. offers juries option of finding defendant both guilty and mentally ill	11. combines M'Naghten with irresistible impulse
8. insane because one cannot tell right from wrong	
9. problem involving recognizing violent tendencies after violence has occured	
10. incorrectly predicting behavior when it does not happen	
12. duty to warn	

MULTIPLE CHOICE

Answers are found at the end of this chapter. The multiple choice questions listed will test your understanding of the material presented in the chapter. Read through each question and circle the letter representing the best answer.

1. A psychologist tells a judge that a person should be hospitalized because they are a threat to themselves. If the judge agrees and hospitalizes the person, we have an example of what kind of commitment?
    a. civil commitment
    b. criminal commitment
    c. legal commitment
    d. voluntary commitment

2. In the GBMI (guilty, but mentally ill) verdict, the defendant
    a. is imprisoned.
    b. can receive treatment.
    c. may stay in prison longer because of the mental illness.
    d. all of the above.

3. Requiring therapists to warn third parties of threats by their clients may increase the risk of violence by their clients because
    a. many violent people do not want to "look bad" by talking about it and not acting on it.
    b. talking about the violent acts may make the person more apt to act on them.
    c. therapists may be less willing to probe their clients about violent tendencies.
    d. the client is very likely to direct the violence toward the therapist.

4. The following might be an example of a post hoc problem:
    a. Difficulty in coming to a consensus of how to define "dangerousness."
    b. Noticing the "red flags" of the suspects' past dangerous behaviors in the Columbine High School shooting in Littleton, Colorado following the rampage.
    c. a and b.
    d. None of the above.

5. According to a recent study on patients' right to refuse treatment, hospitalized patients who refused medication tended to:
    a. be more assaultive
    b. be more compliant with other treatment options
    c. have shorter hospital stays
    d. b & c

6. Accuracy in predicting potential violence in a client is improved when they are based on
    a. client self-report.
    b. the client's behavior while hospitalized.
    c. the client's past community behavior.
    d. client self-report corroborated with reports from individuals who know the client well.

7. What happens if a person is found incompetent to stand trial?
   a. They are found guilty but mentally ill and confined to a prison.
   b. They are confined in a mental institution until they become competent.
   c. They are immediately confined to a mental institution for life.
   d. They are found not guilty by reason of insanity.

8. Thomas Szasz believes that the insanity defense is degrading to defendants because it assumes that people
   a. have free choice.
   b. lack personal responsibility.
   c. have personal determination.
   d. are guilty until proven innocent.

9. In Addington v. Texas, the United States Supreme Court ruled that a person can be involuntarily hospitalized
   a. if they are "mentally ill" alone.
   b. if they are a danger to themselves or others alone.
   c. a and b.
   d. none of the above.

10. The American Law Institute (ALI) guidelines to define insanity make the decision of juries _____ because it _____ the number of cases in which the insanity plea could be used.
   a. harder; increases
   b. harder; decreases
   c. easier; increases
   d. easier; decreases

11. Which of the following must take place before an individual can be involuntarily placed in a psychiatric setting?
   a. A formal commitment petition must be filed with the court.
   b. A complete psychiatric evaluation must be completed on the individual.
   c. The individual must be currently engaged in treatment.
   d. The individual must be deemed as a threat to themselves or others.

12. One of the implications of the Tarasoff case is that
   a. it ended the principle of therapist-client confidentiality.
   b. it created the principle of therapist-client confidentiality.
   c. it requires the therapists to breach therapist-client confidentiality.
   d. it requires that clients assume the responsibility for asking therapists about the limits of confidentiality.

13. Thomas Szasz has suggested which of the following?
    a. Mental illness reflects an underlying medical problem.
    b. People should not be deprived of their freedom simply because they appear to be different.
    c. While the mental patient is dangerous; society may also be dangerous.
    d. Mentally ill people who violate the law should go free because they are not responsible.

14. In general, the percentage of patients who actually refuse medication is
    a. one percent.
    b. five percent.
    c. ten percent.
    d. twenty percent.

15. Persons released from mental hospitals often require
    a. affordable housing.
    b. alcohol abuse counseling.
    c. social services.
    d. all of the above.

16. All of the following are considered rights of the patient according to "The Patient's Bill of Rights under Wyatt v. Stickney," except
    a. nutritionally balanced diets.
    b. suitable opportunities to interact with the opposite gender.
    c. visitation and telephone privileges.
    d. all of the above.

17. In the case of Donaldson v. O'Connor, Kenneth Donaldson, the plaintiff in the case, was institutionalized by his father and
    a. was provided with only occupational training while institutionalized.
    b. refused medication while institutionalized.
    c. was aggressively violent toward other members on his ward while institutionalized.
    d. received no treatment whatsoever while institutionalized.

18. Michael Jones was caught shoplifting, a crime with a maximum punishment of one year in prison. He was found not guilty by reason of insanity and
    a. was released immediately.
    b. was confined to a hospital for six months.
    c. was confined to a hospital for one year.
    d. was still confined to a hospital seven years after the crime occurred.

19. The rights of patients to refuse psychotropic medications was tested in which of the following cases?
    a. Durham v. United States
    b. Rogers v. Okin
    c. Jones v. United States
    d. Medina v. California

20. Professionals overpredict violence in people with abnormal behavior because
    a. they readily agree on what behavior is violent and dangerous.
    b. behavior in hospital settings provide a good indicator for behavior in the community.
    c. hospitalized individuals frequently issue specific threats to others.
    d. violent acts in hospitals and society are relatively rare.

21. The first insanity defense in history established that a person was not guilty because of
    a. irresistible impulses due to a mental illness.
    b. the inability to tell right from wrong.
    c. the inability to understand the crime.
    d. both a and c.

SHORT ANSWER
Answers are found at the end of this chapter. Answer the following short answer questions:

1.   Under what conditions can a person be involuntarily hospitalized?
2.   What rights does a patient who has been committed have?
3.   How successful are professionals in predicting dangerousness? What factors limit their ability to predict dangerous behavior?
4.   What is the "duty to warn"? What landmark case established the duty? What concerns have therapists raised about the duty to warn?
5.   What is the legal basis for the insanity defense?

ANSWERS TO MATCHING

1. civil commitment (p. 538)

2. M'Naghten rule (p. 548)

3. base-rate problem (p. 541)

4. Jones v. United States (p. 550)

5. voluntary hospitalization (p. 538)

6. competent to stand trial (p. 551)

7. O'Connor v. Donaldson (p. 544)

8. Durham v. United States (p. 548)

9. legal commitment (p. 538)

10. false negative (p. 541)

11. Medina v. California (p. 552)

12. Tarasoff v. Regents of the University of California (p. 542)

13. Ali Guideline (p. 549)

14. Youngberg v. Romero (p. 545)

15. insanity defense (p. 547)

16. false positive (p. 541)

17. Wyatt v. Stickney (p. 542)

18. Rogers v. Okin (p. 546)

19. Addington v. Texas (p. 538)

20. post hoc problem (p. 540)

21. duty to war (p. 542)

22. GBMI (pp. 547, 548)

ANSWERS TO MULTIPLE CHOICE QUESTIONS

1. a. civil commitment (p. 538)

2. d. all of the above. (pp. 547, 548)

3. d. the client is very likely to direct the violence toward the therapist. (p. 543)

4. b. noticing the "red flags" of the suspects' past dangerous behaviors in the Columbine High School shooting in Littleton, Colorado following the rampage. (p. 540)

5. a. be more assaultive. (p. 546)

6. c. the client's past community behavior. (p. 540)

7. b. They are confined to a mental institution until they become competent. (pp. 551, 552)

8. b. lack personal responsibility. (pp. 538-539; p. 551)

9. c. a and b. (p. 538)

10. a. harder; increases (p. 549)

11. d. The individual must be deemed as a threat to themselves or others. (p. 538)

12. c. it requires the therapists to breach therapist/client confidentiality. (pp. 542, 543)

13. b. people should not be deprived of their freedom simply because they appear to be different (p. 538)

14. c. ten percent. (p. 546)

15. d. all of the above. (p. 537)

16. d. all of the above. (p. 542)

17. d. received no treatment whatsoever while institutionalized. (p. 544)

18. d. was still confined to a hospital seven years after the crime occurred (p. 550)

19. b. Rogers v. Okin (p. 546)

20. d. violent acts in hospitals and society are relatively rare. (p. 541)

21. b. the inability to tell right from wrong. (p. 548)

ANSWERS TO SHORT ANSWER QUESTIONS

1. In order for individuals to be involuntarily hospitalized, they must be judged to be both 'mentally ill' and to present a clear and present danger to themselves or to others (Addington v. Texas). Legal placement of individuals against their will is called civil commitment. Civil commitment typically requires a petition be filed by a family member or professional. Psychiatric examiners may then be empowered by the court system to evaluate the individual and provide testimony. (p. 538)

2. Minimum standards of patient care were established in the case of Wyatt v. Stickney in 1972. Psychiatric hospitals must, at a minimum, provide a humane psychological and physical environment, qualified staff, and individualized treatment plans. Furthermore, the patient has a right to privacy, a right to be treated with dignity and under the least restrictive conditions, a right to visitation, a right to refuse excessive and unnecessary medication, a right to refuse potentially hazardous treatment, a right to exercise and suitable opportunities to interact with others, and a right to humane living conditions and a nutritionally balanced diet. The patient also may not be subjected to experimental treatment, unless informed consent rights are protected, and must not be subjected to restraint or isolation except for emergency situations. (pp. 542-544)

3. Professionals have not been very successful in predicting dangerousness. Mental health professionals who have relied on clinical judgment have not been very accurate in predicting dangerousness in the clients they treat. The factors limiting professionals in their ability to predict dangerousness include the post hoc problem, the problem in leaping from the general to the specific, the problem in defining dangerousness, the base-rate problem, the unlikelihood of disclosure of direct threats of violence, and the difficulty in predicting behavior in the community from behavior in the hospital. It is much easier to understand the factors that have lead to a violent incident after an incident has occurred (post hoc) than to predict a violent incident (ad hoc). General tendencies toward violence do not equate to specific acts, as not all individuals who display such tendencies act upon them. Furthermore, there is lack of agreement in defining criteria for labeling behavior as dangerous. Definitions are often based upon sociopolitical factors and the context in which one lives. The base-rate problem involves the relative difficulty in making predictions of infrequent events such as violent acts. It is also unlikely that truly dangerous individuals will disclose their intentions to mental health professional prior to their actions. Finally, violent or dangerous behavior observed in a hospital setting does not always transfer to the community. Dangerous behavior may be situation specific, leading to significant difficulty in predicting such behavior. (pp. 548, 549)

4. The duty to warn is a therapist's obligation to warn third parties of threats made against them by clients. Tarasoff v. Regents of the University of California was the landmark case that established the duty. In 1969, a university of California graduate student murdered Tatiana Tarasoff. The student informed his psychologist prior to the murder of his intent to kill Tarasoff. Although the psychologist consulted colleagues and notified the police, Tarasoff was not informed. Concerns regarding the duty to warn stem from rights to confidentiality within a therapeutic context. Whereas the intent of the decision was to protect potential victims, individuals may be less willing to enter into therapy or confide in their therapist as the result of the duty. Moreover, therapists may be less likely to probe violent tendencies for fear of legal complications. (pp. 542, 543)

5. There are three major court rulings that bear on the insanity defense. First is a case in Ohio in 1834 in which it was ruled that individuals could not be held responsible if the crime was the result of impulses they could not resist. The second is the M'Naghten rule, based upon a case in England in 1843, in which it was decreed that individuals are not criminally responsible if they have no knowledge of their actions or are not able to distinguish right from wrong as the result of a mental defect or disease. The third major case, Durham v. United States, holds that an accused individual is not criminally responsible if the criminal act was the result of a mental disease or mental defect. Under the Durham rule, juries were expected to decide whether the accused suffered from a mental disease or defect and whether the disease or defect caused the criminal act. In 1972, legal guidelines formulated by the American Law Institute replaced the Durham rule and combined the M'Naghten rule with irresistible impulse principles. (pp. 548, 549)